Interest Groups

COMPARATIVE POLITICS

Edited by Gillian Peele
Lady Margaret Hall, Oxford

Forthcoming:

Colin Campbell, SJ *Bureaucracies*

John Francis *Regulation*

Bruce Graham *Representation and Party Politics*

Philip Norton *Legislatures*

B. Guy Peters *The Politics of Taxation*

Interest Groups

Graham K. Wilson

Basil Blackwell

Copyright © Graham K. Wilson 1990

First published 1990

Basil Blackwell Ltd
108 Cowley Road, Oxford, OX4 1JF, UK

Basil Blackwell, Inc.
3 Cambridge Center
Cambridge, Massachusetts 02142, USA

British Library Cataloguing in Publication Data

A CIP catalogue record for this book is available from the British Library.

Library of Congress Cataloging in Publication Data

Wilson, Graham K.
    Interest groups / Graham K. Wilson.
      p. cm. — (Comparative politics)
    Includes bibliographical references.
    ISBN 0-631-16051-5 ISBN 0-631-17446-X (pbk.)
    1. Pressure groups. 2. Comparative government. I. Title.
  II. Series: Comparative politics (Oxford, England)
JF529.W55 1990   89-28287
324'.4—dc20   CIP

Typeset in 11 on 13 pt Sabon
by Photo·graphics, Honiton, Devon
Printed in Great Britain by T.J. Press Ltd, Padstow

Contents

For Gina and Adam,
my most real and lasting interests

Preface to the Series

This new series in comparative politics has been designed with three broad objectives in mind. In the first instance it is hoped that, by focusing on a number of contemporary themes and issues in comparative politics, the individual studies may cumulatively make a contribution to the subject. Comparative politics has never been an easy discipline; and the subject has become more difficult as conceptual approaches have proliferated and the weight of material available to scholars has increased. As a result there has been a certain fragmentation as the task of refining the conceptualization has become separated from the detailed studies of institutions and political processes across political systems.

This tendency for discussions of the framework of comparative politics to become divorced from the subject's empirical research agenda has certainly been debilitating for the discipline. But it has also been misleading for the student. A second aim of the series is therefore to fill a gap in the literature by providing volumes which will combine empirical and theoretical material in easily accessible form. Each study will introduce the student to the current debates between political scientists about the major issues involved in the comparative study of a particular subject. However, each study will also deploy sufficient information drawn from a range of political systems to enable the reader to evaluate those debates for himself.

A third goal of the series is to take account of recent political developments which make it necessary to look at governmental systems in new ways. The enhanced importance of supra-national institutions (such as the European Community) and the resurgence of free market doctrines are but two examples of changes in the political landscape which have major implications for the organization of government in a number of states. Thus, in addition to the familiar canon of topics in comparative politics, the series will contain studies which explore themes which are perhaps less frequently handled in a comparative manner. The series will contain volumes on such central subjects as legislatures and pressure groups; but studies which examine taxation, regulation and the politicization of bureaucracies have also been commissioned.

Although this series has been designed with clear goals in mind, the individual authors have been allowed to exercise their judgement about which countries to include in their discussions. The only requirement is that they should provide an introduction both to the theoretical debates about their chosen theme and to the way the issue presents itself in the context of modern government.

The first volume in the series is one which displays the goals of the series admirably. Graham Wilson, whose teaching career has been truly transatlantic, examines the role of interest groups in modern political systems. Interest groups are important not only because of the way they affect public policy but also because of the role they play in linking the institutions of the state to society. Graham Wilson points to the impact which recent intellectual developments (such as the rise of public choice theory and concern with the role of the state) have had on theoretical discussions about interest groups. At the same time, he underlines the extent to which continuing doubts about the definition of power and how best to assess whether or not a group is influential have bedevilled the study of interest groups.

Although Professor Wilson provides a comprehensive overview of these arguments, he does not allow them to blur his perspective on the more empirical aspects of his subject. For, as he emphasizes, the fact is that interest groups are a pervasive phenomenon in modern political systems and there is much to be learnt by focusing on the different resources and styles of these groups across a range of countries.

A substantial portion of any examination of interest groups is bound to devote considerable attention to the United States. Nor is this surprising. The role of organized interests in the USA has generated an extensive literature on all aspects of the relationship between groups and the wider democratic system. However, as

Professor Wilson points out, in many respects American interest groups are as idiosyncratic as American political parties and, while the student of comparative politics must take the American experience into account, it would be a mistake to generalize too much from the American pattern. Professor Wilson's own research and publications display extensive knowledge of the policy process in a number of sectors and a number of political systems. I am extremely pleased, therefore, that this book should be the first in the series to be published. I feel sure that it will prove invaluable to all concerned with the comparative study of government and politics.

Gillian Peele
Lady Margaret Hall
Oxford

Preface

The last ten years have surely been one of the most exciting periods in interest group studies. A number of new perspectives and approaches have carried the study of interest groups and politics to a new level. A wealth of studies of interest groups outside the USA has made us aware that the interest groups of the USA, far from being exemplars as had been supposed, are just as idiosyncratic as American political parties. A convergence between 'mainstream' writers, some like Dahl and Lindblom, once leading proponents of the dominant pluralist tradition but now more critical of the approach, and neo-marxist writers, more interested in dialogue and empirical research than previously, has made possible an unusually stimulating discussion of how government and the major interests in society connect. The movement to 'bring the state back in' to political science has raised many questions for students of interest groups which have yet to be fully stated let alone answered. Another group of writers, the rational choice theorists, have brought their considerable talents to bear on the study of the formation, maintenance and impact of interest groups using techniques essentially borrowed from micro-economics. Although I am more doubtful than many about the ultimate value of rational choice approaches, it cannot be denied that work in that tradition has posed major challenges and questions for the rest of the discipline.

This book is my attempt to look at interest group politics comparatively. The value of the comparative perspective is that it makes one aware of what is commonplace and what is unique in any political system. The sense of what is unique and what is commonplace in any political system seems to me to be so valuable for political scientists that it is worth paying a high cost to pursue it. Undoubtedly there is a cost. The volume of research in political science today makes it harder than ever to master the state of knowledge on any single country. Those of us who try to take a broad perspective must ask the indulgence of experts on those countries about which our knowledge is weaker. I have seen experts on single countries labour hard to produce explanations for developments within their country so often without realizing that the phenomenon they are analysing has close counterparts in other countries which their explanation does not fit; for that reason I think it important to take the risks of a comparative approach.

I have been fortunate in spending part of my career in two countries and in two fine political science departments, Essex and Wisconsin. I have realized that many of the people who have influenced my thinking the most are people whose ideas I thought initially I was rejecting. I owe special debts, however, to Gillian Peele for her comments on my manuscript and to my wife, Virginia Sapiro, whose intelligence, loyalty and love support my work and life.

Graham K. Wilson
University of Wisconsin
Madison

1

On Studying Interest Groups

One of the fundamental concerns of political scientists of all traditions is the achievement of an understanding of the relationship between the state and society. Definitions of the state differ considerably. Yet common to most traditions of thinking about the state are questions about its relationship to society in general. Which interests does government or the state serve? How much freedom of action or autonomy from society does the state enjoy? Political scientists do not agree on the answers to these questions; indeed, the answers may vary from one point in history to another, or one nation to another. The study of interest groups appears, however, to promise much in trying to answer these questions.

Interest groups are generally defined as organizations, separate from government though often in close partnership with government, which attempt to influence public policy. As such, interest groups provide the institutionalized linkage between government or the state and major sectors of society. A random sampling of the activities or policies of interest groups in any western society would produce a list containing a most remarkable variety of concerns including issues as diverse as contraception, food hygiene, international trade policy, nuclear defence strategy and the protection of areas of natural beauty or listed buildings. As those who have defended the contribution of interest groups to democratic politics have noted, interest groups raise issues and articulate needs far more diverse than can be presented or discussed by political parties. Much of the organized interaction between government and the numerous interests in society takes place through interest groups; the study of interest groups is thus of major importance in understanding the relationship between state and society.

Yet the study of interest groups often involves more passion than the study of other political institutions such as parliamentary or congressional committees. Interest groups have an unusual normative significance which arouses passions. A variety of issues raised about interest groups in political theory contributes to the significance of interest group studies.

First, in the tradition of Rousseau[1] and, on closer inspection than his views on interest groups often receive, Madison,[2] we might fear that interest groups will warp public policy by asserting minority rights or opinions against the interests or opinions of the majority. The implications of Rousseau's concern to secure the triumph of the general will consistent with the interests of all and not merely the interests of a sector of society have been widely discussed by political theorists. Rousseau's antipathy to interest groups will find support today among many observers of political life.

If the people, engaged in deliberation, were adequately informed, and if no means existed by which the citizens could communicate one with another, from the great number of small differences the general will would result and the decisions reached would always be good. But when intriguing groups and partial associations are formed to the disadvantage of the whole, then the will of each of such groups is general only in respect of its own members, but partial in respect of the State.

The possible conflict between liberty and the pursuit of the general will implicit in Rousseau's view is even starker in another passage from *The Social Contract*. 'If, then, the general will is to be truly expressed, it is essential that there be no subsidiary groups within the State, and that each citizen voice his own opinion and nothing but his own opinion.' However, if groups cannot be prevented, they should be as numerous as possible in order to limit their effect: 'where subsidiary groups do exist their numbers should be

---

[1] Jean-Jacques Rousseau, *The Social Contract* (with an introduction by Sir Ernest Barker), Oxford University Press, Oxford and New York, 1968.
[2] Alexander Hamilton, James Madison and John Jay, *The Federalist Papers*, Willmoore Kendall and George Carey (eds), Arlington House, New Rochelle, 1966. See also Gary Wills, *Explaining America*, Doubleday, Garden City, New York, 1966.

made as large as possible and none should be more powerful than its fellows.'[3]

Rousseau's conclusion was not so different, therefore, from that of James Madison, sometimes cited as an enthusiast for interest group politics. It is often forgotten that Madison's acceptance of the ubiquity of interest groups or factions was based on the hope expressed in *Federalist Papers* 10 and 51 that selfish interest groups would hold each other in check so that we might turn to a consideration of policies which would serve the common good. Madison's belief in the superiority of large over small political systems (contrasting with Rousseau's belief in the superiority of small countries) was based in large part on his argument that sources of countervailing power against an otherwise dominating interest could be more readily found in large than in small systems. However successful might be the solutions proposed by political theorists, the fear that interest groups will subvert the common interest or block the wishes of a majority remains. Such fears continue to give zest to discussion of interest groups.

A second theme in political theory focuses on the possibility that interest groups can temper the majoritarian failings of democracy. Theorists such as the great French observer of the United States in the 1830s, Alexis de Tocqueville, whose work[4] warned eloquently of the possibility of a 'tyranny of the majority' in democratic systems under which the views or interests of minorities will be sacrificed, have found some consolation – like Tocqueville himself – in interest groups. Interest groups not only provide an alternative form of political participation to voting or membership of a political party but in certain respects they may provide a superior form of participation. Interest groups are useful in that they raise issues too detailed or specialized to be the concern of political parties or central in election campaigns. More importantly, interest groups allow 'intense minorities', groups vitally affected by a policy issue, to prevail over majorities to whom the issue matters little. As the great American political scientist, Robert Dahl, noted,[5] interest groups might thus correct

---

[3] Rousseau, *The Social Contract*, p. 194.

[4] Alexis de Tocqueville, *De la Démocratie en Amérique*, Bordas, Paris, 1973.

[5] Robert Dahl, *A Preface to Democratic Theory*, University of Chicago Press, Chicago, 1956.

one of the alleged defects of democratic politics in allocating resources compared with the allocation of resources through market mechanisms, that it takes no account of the intensity of desires. A determined campaign by a minority interest group which overcomes a relatively indifferent majority may be the political equivalent of the market system facilitating the provision of a good on which a minority are prepared to spend a significant proportion of their incomes.

A third theme expressed by the classic theorists was that interest groups would serve a useful purpose by providing a mediating structure standing between the state and the citizen. The mediating role of interest groups may serve to protect citizens from intimidation by the state. Whereas the enormous contrast between the power of the state and the powerlessness of the individual might destroy freedom, individuals allied in interest groups may be better able to defend themselves. Interest groups might also provide training grounds for citizenship in which the skills and values of democratic politics can be learnt.[6] The smaller scale and friendlier climate of an interest group might encourage individuals to develop confidence in their political skills or efficacy which could then be translated to the larger stage of electoral politics. Moreover, participation in interest groups might inculcate respect for democratic values such as debate, or tolerance of the views of others. Writers who feared the alienating aspects of modern mass societies in particular revived the idea of interest groups as institutions which could integrate the individual into society because they were mediating institutions between the small individual and the vast scale of most modern institutions.[7]

The apotheosis of the optimistic interpretation of interest groups is *pluralism*. Pluralism has had both prescriptive and descriptive characteristics. Prescriptively, pluralism has combined arguments outlined above in defence of interest group politics to argue that interest groups are a desirable, even indispensable, part of modern democracy. When critics of pluralism as prescriptive doctrine have asked who cares for the common good or general interest in a pluralist system, pluralists have replied that the common

---

[6] This was of course a central theme in Tocqueville, *De la Démocratie.*
[7] Alan Kornberg, *The Politics of Mass Society*, The Free Press, Glencoe, 1959.

good or general interest either is merely the sum of the interests of different groups in society or is non-existent, there being no common, public or national interest, merely different interpret- ations or views of what is desirable public policy.

The sharpest debates between pluralists and their critics have concerned the *descriptive* accuracy of pluralism, however. Before a society could be said to be pluralist, certain conditions would have to be met. First, all sectors of society would have to be represented within the interest group system, or would be able to develop an interest group reasonably easily if they wished to be represented by one. Second, power should be distributed reasonably equally between groups. Certainly no one group should be able to control or dominate policymaking, and in contrast, all groups should have a significant opportunity to shape or influence public policy. Pluralists initially stated or implied that certain nations, notably the United States, had attained, or were very close to attaining, pluralism. In contrast, critics of the pluralists argued that there was a large gap between current political reality in the United States and other western democracies and the pluralist ideal. Some sectors of society, such as the poor, lacked the resources to form interest groups, while vital general interests (for example, in clean air or water) were poorly represented. In contrast, some groups, and in particular business, enjoyed a variety of advantages which allowed them to dominate the policy process. After decades of such criticism, leading pluralists such as Dahl and Charles Lindblom revised their views somewhat acknowledging that the impediments to pluralism were greater than they had suggested initially, and that determined radical reforms might be necessary before current democracies attained pluralism. The debate between pluralists and their critics about the degree to which existing political systems could be called pluralist has dominated writing on interest groups for over three decades and engaged many of the best-known political scientists.

The publication of the early works of pluralists such as Dahl encouraged the belief that the study of interest groups would be a major element in research in political science.[8] Yet in spite of,

---

[8] David Truman, *The Governmental Process*, Alfred Knopf, New York, 1951. G. David Garson, *Group Theories of Politics*, Sage Publications, Beverly Hills, 1978.

or perhaps because of, the importance of the controversy between pluralists and their critics, empirical research on interest groups stagnated. There were no doubt many reasons for this stagnation, including the findings of empirical studies which suggested that the impact of interest groups on public policy was modest and the growth of alternative areas of study, such as voting behaviour. A major reason for the stagnation of interest group studies, however, was the conceptual fog originating in the debate between pluralists and their critics which enveloped the field and the consequent confusion which developed not only about the conclusions to be drawn from research on interest groups but also about the methods and assumptions which should guide the study of interest groups. An appreciation of the issues involved is essential for an understanding of what interest group studies can, and cannot, contribute.

Definitional Problems and Traps

One of the most basic problems for interest group studies is the problem of definition. Some organizations are clearly what we should understand an interest group to be. Such organizations recruit members with the explicit promise that the organization will pursue certain public policy goals. People who join the League Against Cruel Sports in Britain or Common Cause in the United States are clearly joining together to support an organization which is obviously dedicated to certain relatively well-defined public policy objectives and would be agreed by all observers to be joining an interest group whose primary purpose was influencing public policy in favour of those objectives. Few organizations commonly regarded as interest groups are like the League or Common Cause. Most organizations which participate in interest group politics do not recruit individuals with the promise to represent their views or interests politically. General Motors and Shell frequently urge their views or interests on government and therefore engage in interest group activities. Yet corporations do not recruit members or even make clear their political views to shareholders or employees. Similarly, unions recruit members by promising to secure better working conditions or wages. Yet unions are heavily engaged in promoting a wide range of policies which may or may not have the support of their members. Professional organizations such as the British Medical Association (BMA) or American Medical Association (AMA) though heavily involved in lobbying exist primarily to provide other services to their members. Are we to conclude that any organization which seeks to any degree to influence public policy is therefore to be regarded as an interest group? If not, how much political activity is required before an organization which exists for some other purpose may be regarded as an interest group?

Similarly, some writers have argued that not all interest groups are organizations.[9] Writers focusing on social movements, for example, have argued that both those active in any way in support of the movement and even those in the population sharing the relevant characteristics of the movement should be understood as members of the interest group. Thus it is common in the United States to talk of both women and blacks as interest groups even though the differences of attitude and circumstance amongst these groups are enormous. Some of the 1950s' writers on interest group politics even extended the term to cover quasi-groups, interest groups which had yet to form but which might in the future given sufficient stimulus to do so. Interest groups are defined therefore simply as sectors of society or groups of people who might be said to share a common interest.

Anyone is always free to stipulate a definition he/she likes for any term he/she chooses. It is up to the rest of us to decide whether or not that definition is helpful. Many studies of interest groups have defined the term narrowly, and have focused only on membership organizations. Such a narrow definition of interest groups would have the peculiar effect of excluding large businesses such as ICI or Du Pont from our view, surely a strange and unwelcome outcome.[10] Broad definitions of interest groups also have their problems. To argue that large blocks of the population (e.g., the young, the old, women) constitute interest groups is to

[9] For an able statement of this view, see Virginia Sapiro, 'When are interests interesting?', *APSR*, 75, 3 (1981), pp. 701–16.

[10] Jack Walker, 'The origins and maintenance of interest groups in America', *APSR*, 77, 2 (1983), pp. 390–406. See in contrast Kay Lehman Schlozman and John Tierney, *Organized Interests and American Democracy*, Harper and Row, New York, 1986. Schlozman and Tierney deliberately avoid the term 'interest group' in their title so as to be more encompassing.

argue that the common interest which unites the group is of much greater importance than the factors (e.g., wealth, region, race) which divide the groups, an argument which may represent more the beliefs of the observer than reality. The relationship between an interest group and an allied or sympathetic social movement is often very complex, as the examples of the women's movement and groups such as the National Organization for Women (NOW) in the United States demonstrate. While some in the women's movement see NOW as the natural institutionalization of their activity, others see NOW as irrelevant or even damaging to the concerns of the movement because an interest group inevitably adapts to the existing power structure. Without discussing the truth or falseness of these claims, they do serve to illustrate the desirability of keeping, conceptually, different sectors of the population, social movements and interest groups separate. By requiring that for something to be an interest group, it must have an institutionalized existence I distinguish interest groups from social movements (which need have only the most rudimentary linkages) and avoid the problem of specifying which groups in society have sufficient in common to be called an interest group in spite of differences within the group.

My approach in defining interest groups has been to rely on the requirements that interest groups be *organizations* which have some autonomy from government or political parties and that they try to influence public policy. The degree to which interest groups can be distinguished from government and political parties will be discussed below. Suffice to say here that one advantage of a comparative perspective on interest groups is that it makes it clear that in practice the degree of separation between interest groups and either government or political parties varies considerably, often amounting to comparatively little. Interest groups may well have extremely close links to either parties or government and may well offer or be required to administer policy on behalf of governments. At times, interest groups such as the (American) National Farmers' Union or United Auto Workers (UAW) have come close to being to all intents and purposes the Democratic Party in certain areas of the United States. In Detroit, for example, the UAW was able to determine which candidate received the Democratic Party nomination and provided the money, volunteers and organization to run the campaign thereafter. The National

Farmers' Union played a vital role in the emergence of the Democratic Party in the upper Midwest (Minnesota, North Dakota and South Dakota) in the 1950s, prior to which the area had been in the hands of Republicans of one ideological character or another more or less exclusively. In countries such as Sweden or Japan, interest groups gain their importance in large part because of the close partnership they have forged with government in the development and implementation of policy. Yet even in Japan and Sweden, the state has its boundaries; the highly influential LO (Landsorganatsionen, Swedish Federation of Labour) or Keidanren (the Federation of Economic Organizations, i.e., the Japanese employers' organization) are not mistaken for parts of government.

Such a definition also allows for one of the most important aspects of interest group politics in certain countries, namely its fluidity. A given organization may not be functioning as an interest group this year but may be next year. A corporation or a university may be politically inactive in one period and yet vigorously involved in lobbying in another period. It is precisely my intent to say that the organization in question without changing its fundamental character changes into an interest group as it is politicized. Similarly, a social movement may or may not become an interest group depending on whether or not it develops the appropriate degree of institutionalization. In the United States, the upsurge of protest among farmers in the late nineteenth century left behind an interest group still functioning today (the Grange); discontent among workers in mass production industries gave birth (with government help) to the 'industrial unions', such as the United Auto Workers or the Steelworkers; and the National Organization for Women is a permanent feature of the Washington scene, even if the women's movement were to decline. In contrast, some social movements have left us with a much lesser institutional legacy. The Progressive Movement, for example, left little institutional legacy, although it can be argued that the public interest groups of the 1970s became heirs to its traditions. The degrees to which interest groups are supported by or grow out of social movements, participate in electoral politics or take in what might be thought to be functions of government (e.g., in policy implementation) are appropriate areas for research which should not be blocked by definitions of interest groups which are so broad as to blur distinctions between interest groups and these other political phenomena.

If it has been hard to define interest groups, it is even harder to reach any consensus about their importance. The most important single question motivating research on interest groups was the question of the collective and relative power of interest groups. As the foremost normative question about interest groups concerns their ability to subvert the common good or to block majority opinion, it was natural that the power of interest groups should be of great concern for empirical research. Were interest groups collectively so powerful that public policy would be the sum of the wishes of interest groups, perhaps, as Schattschneider argued[11] in the case of American trade policy between the wars, to the detriment of the public interest? Was a single interest, perhaps business, so effectively represented by interest groups that it was able to shape public policies which concerned it? Were western governments, as the overload theorists argued in the late 1970s (and whose theories are discussed below), so harried by interest groups that ungovernability was nigh? Such questions have always been a driving force in research on interest groups.

Unfortunately, there has been little agreement not only on the answers to such questions but on what would constitute an answer. The practical problems of research are severe enough. Take the example of a Member of Parliament who votes against allowing shops to open on Sundays in Britain in 1987. Is the MP's vote due to the fact that the religious sabbatarians have exerted as much pressure on parliament as they could, or to the MP's own beliefs, or to the fear of losing support in the constituency or to pressures from other MPs? Even if the MP knows the answer, it is doubtful if many will admit, were it to be true, that their vote had been cast as a result of pressure from an interest group. An analogous problem exists for those conducting research on the effects of campaign contributions by interest groups in the United States.[12] Legislators are hardly likely to admit that they have sold their vote to an interest group in

---

[11] E. E. Schattschneider, *Politics, Pressures and the Tariff*, Arno Press, New York, 1974 (original 1935).

[12] For a useful summary of research on this issue, see Larry Sabato, *PAC Power*, Norton, New York, 1984.

return for a campaign contribution but will instead justify a vote in terms of their beliefs, the opinions of constituents or the consequences of the legislation for the prosperity of the district or state. Moreover, even if it could be shown in certain areas that interest groups had played a major role in influencing policy, as Theodore Lowi has noted,[13] it would almost certainly be a mistake to generalize that conclusion to different policy areas. Lowi has argued that there are three different types of policy area – the redistributive, distributive and regulatory. Redistributive policies transfer resources from one large group in society (e.g., the rich) to another (e.g., the poor). Distributive policies share out benefits among many different regions or districts, a classic example being public works projects promoted by a log-rolling coalition in the American Congress, every supporter getting a project for his or her district. Regulatory policies are typified by environmental controls or limits on price increases by utilities such as telephone companies. Each policy type generates its own unique type of politics; contrary to the usual way of thinking, Lowi suggests that policy shapes politics, rather than that politics shapes policy. Interest groups will be more important in distributive or regulatory policy issues than in redistributive issues, in which broader forces (e.g., political parties) will be more significant. Similarly, James Q. Wilson has distinguished between different types of regulatory policy. James Wilson argues that the *intensity* of the impact of a regulation combined with the *extent* of its impact will shape the type of politics generated. The politics of a regulation which costs a large number of people very little and generates modest benefits for an equally large number will be very different from the politics of a regulation which costs a small number a lot, and benefits a small number a lot. James Wilson concludes that interest group activity is most likely to develop when costs and benefits are concentrated on a small number and are also significant.[14] In brief, the researcher confronts the problem that the extent and importance of interest group activity might be quite different in one policy area than in another.

Yet more fundamentally, interest group studies have been

---

[13] Theodore Lowi, 'American Business, Public Policy, Case Studies and Political Theory', *World Politics* XVI (1964), 4, pp. 677–93.

[14] James Q. Wilson, (ed.), *The Politics of Regulation*, Basic Books, New York, 1983.

bedevilled by the lack of agreement among political scientists on the definition of power. Quite simply, political scientists have not agreed on what is properly included or excluded in studying the power of an interest group. Everyone would agree that the overt forms of political activity are relevant. Helping political parties or candidates win elections by supplying money, votes or campaign workers may be supposed to predispose the parties or candidates in favour of interest groups which supply such help. Are there, however, less obvious forms of power which may in fact be more important in explaining which interest groups are the most powerful? Public opinion (or the dominant ideology as some would term it) might be so prejudiced against unions in the United States that their extensive commitment to overt political action would be of limited value. The question of whether or not the power of business can be explained within the framework of conventional studies of interest groups has been particularly troublesome. The ability of financial institutions in the City of London to transfer billions of pounds overseas in seconds may be a more powerful influence were there to be a Labour government than the representations of interest groups speaking for those financial institutions. American states and even nations make major efforts today to improve their 'business climates' by cutting taxes on corporations and their executives, by easing regulations affecting business and by offering subsidies for new developments. All this is done not because of interest group activity, such as making campaign contributions or particularly astute lobbying by business executives, but because states, nations or cities know their future prosperity is dependent on attracting investment which can easily be switched to another city, state or, in the age of the multinational corporation, to other countries.[15]

Lukes has advanced the somewhat gloomy view that power is an essentially contested concept, i.e., a concept which cannot

---

[15] The 1960s and 1970s produced important literature on the meaning or nature of power. Among the most important works were: Robert Dahl, *Who Governs?*, Yale University Press, New Haven, 1961; Peter Bachrach and Morton Baratz, *Power and Poverty; Theory and Practice*, Oxford University Press, Oxford and New York, 1970; Matthew Crenson, *The Un-Politics of Air Pollution, A Study of Non-Decisionmaking in the Cities*, Johns Hopkins University Press, Baltimore and London, 1971; Steven Lukes, *Power, A Radical View*, Macmillan, London, 1974. Charles E. Lindblom, *Politics and Markets, The World's Political Economic Systems*, Basic Books, New York, 1977.

be defined without reference to the very broad political and philosophical beliefs of the person concerned. Marxists and non-marxists will not agree on the definition of power, let alone on whether or not empirically a particular group is or is not powerful. Lukes's pessimism is not shared by all theorists. In practice, however, lack of agreement on method which Lukes describes has helped to fuel the arguments about the relative power of interest groups. In the 1950s and early 1960s pluralist writers concluded, on the basis of empirical studies of interest groups and their participation in policymaking, that power was divided among numerous groups, none of which enjoyed a dominant position. Mainstream political scientists such as Schattschneider and Olson attacked implications that the interest group system was fair. Schattschneider emphasized the much greater representation of higher Socio Economic Status (SES) groups within the interest group system than that enjoyed by lower SES groups.[16] Olson emphasized the difficulty that any group which was concerned with public goods (available to all irrespective of whether or not they belonged to the relevant interest group) would have to overcome.[17] Rational people would not give time or money to an interest group seeking a good such as clean air which, were the interest group to succeed, would be available freely to all. Olson's argument has been so influential that it is discussed in more detail below. We should note here, however, his argument that interests of vital importance are likely to be poorly represented in the interest group system.

More fundamental disagreements with the pluralists, first from radical, then from mainstream, political scientists, rested on disagreements with the pluralists about the nature and bases of the power of interest groups. Critics charged that the pluralists neglected the more veiled forms of political power, focusing on the consequences of the action or behaviour of groups (e.g., lobbying) rather than on structural factors shaping power relations. For example, biases in the culture enhancing the prestige of one group and diminishing that of another, or the power

---

[16] E. E. Schattschneider, *The Semi-Sovereign People*, Holt, Reinhart and Winston, New York, 1960.

[17] Mancur Olson, *The Logic of Collective Action, Public Goods and the Theory of Groups*, Schocken Books, New York, 1968.

business enjoys because of its control of investment did not figure in pluralist analyses. Critics of the pluralists argued that if business were able to convince everyone that 'what is good for General Motors is good for the United States' (which is, incidentally, a slight mis-quotation of a remark made by Eisenhower's Defense Secretary), business will be far more helped than it would be by employing a few more lobbyists in Washington DC. Fears that businesses will move elsewhere if public policy is 'anti-business' can change policies more rapidly than numerous PAC (Political Action Committees) contributions.

It was therefore unconvincing, or even irrelevant, for many radicals that political scientists operating within the same philo-sophical framework as pluralists soon reached the conclusion that the power of interest groups had been exaggerated even in countries such as the United States where conditions seemed favourable to interest group power. Legislators, far from being dominated by lobbyists, enjoyed considerable freedom of action.[18] Indeed, lobbyists were generally reduced to the status of unpaid staff assistants to friendly legislators, rarely contacting let alone persuading or intimidating legislators not already favourably disposed to them. The best strategy for a lobbyist to follow was to build a long-term relationship of trust with a politician or civil servant so that the lobbyist might become a valued source of information. Frequently, however, interest groups remained unimpressive organizations deserving and receiving little respect from politicians.

Thus the entirely understandable focus on the power of pressure groups had seemed to lead interest group studies into a dual impasse. First, as we have seen, no universally acceptable definition of the power of interests was available to guide empirical research. Pluralist scholars based their conclusions on a methodology which assumed that the exercise of power by interest groups would be based on actions or behaviour such as making campaign contributions or attempting to deliver a vote. Radical scholars denied that these activities were particularly important and instead focused on structural factors such as which group benefited from

---

[18] Raymond Bauer, Ithiel de Sola Pool and Lewis Anthony Dexter, *American Business and Public Policy*, Atherton Press, New York, 1963; Lester Milbrath, *The Washington Lobbyists*, Rand McNally, Chicago, 1963.

the dominant ideology, or which group (usually business) had so much economic power that governments would serve their interests without being pressured or lobbied. Second, research conducted within the dominant pluralist framework suggested that interest groups generally enjoyed little power and, it might be concluded, were therefore of little significance for political scientists. Both schools of thought suggested that further work on the activities of interest groups was not worthwhile either because, as radicals argued, the activities of interest groups were a poor guide to the power of interests, or because, as mainstream political scientists had argued, in practice, interest groups had only limited impact on public policy.

Both these sceptical attitudes towards the utility of further research on interest groups were open to challenge. The radical view that certain interests, notably business, were so well protected by ideology or the power to control investment seemed much less plausible in the 1970s than in the 1960s as business was forced – even in the USA – to engage in vigorous interest group activity to stem a tide of public policies, such as stricter regulation, damaging to its interests. The conclusions of mainstream political scientists, that interest groups were comparatively powerless, were also open to challenge. As Lowi had noted, the conclusion that interest groups are unimportant in one policy area does not establish that they are unimportant in all policy areas.[19] Moreover, studies often neglected the *indirect* approach used by interest groups. The often repeated conclusion that legislators were more likely to pay attention to other legislators than to lobbyists neglected the fact that the influential legislator might have been mobilized by lobbyists in the first place or at least be working with them. Moreover, the alleged lack of power of interest groups might not have been an eternal truth but, rather, a product of temporary circumstances. The Washington DC of the 1950s – or, for that matter, the Whitehall of the same period – was a locus of decisionmaking much more insulated from outside pressures than the same places in the 1970s. The insulation of

---

[19] Lowi, 'American Business, Public Policy, Case Studies and Political Theory'; for an application of Lowi designed to reconcile conflicting results of studies of lobbying by linking them to the policy area in question, see Michael Hayes, *Lobbyists and Legislators, A Theory of Political Markets*, Rutgers University Press, New Brunswick, 1986.

American legislators from the power of interest groups depended on factors which have changed since. American legislators were insulated from interest groups in the 1950s by procedural safeguards such as holding committee deliberations in private and by the deeply entrenched loyalty of voters to political parties, a loyalty interest groups were powerless to change.[20] Committee hearings and meetings are now held in public under the watchful eye of lobbyists and more voters are willing to abandon their party identification, at least temporarily, than in the 1950s. Political campaigns were much cheaper to run before paid television advertising became so important and the money for campaigns was raised from relatively few rich individuals, instead of a large proportion (about one third) coming from political action committees.

Doubts today about the validity of research on the power of interest groups conducted as long ago as the 1950s can obviously be settled by further research. The continuing barrier to progress in the study of the power of interest groups was the lack of agreement on the meaning of power. If little knowledge of the relative power of business, labour, consumers and environmentalists could be gained by studying their interest group organizations, because the true distribution of power was shaped by sociological rather than overtly political factors, why bother to study interest groups? Admittedly, very few if any major interests in society feel they can do without interest groups to represent them. But it is inconceivable that a radical scholar such as Lukes, focusing on alleged biases in the dominant ideology or the structural power resulting from the ability to make investment decisions, and a mainstream political scientist, trained to focus on observable behaviour as the means of discovering the power of an interest group, would agree on *how* to determine what proportion of the power of business was due to interest group activity, and what proportion to its structural advantages.

Yet however understandable the fascination with the power of

---

[20] For discussions of the extent of change in the American and British political systems by the late 1970s and early 1980s, see Anthony King (ed.), *The New American Political System*, American Enterprise Institute, Washington DC, 1978; Ian Budge, David McKay et al., *The New British Political System, Government and Society in the Eighties*, Longman, London and New York, 1983.

interest groups, it can be questioned whether this was an appropriate question for political scientists to adopt as their original concern. No area of political science has made much progress when its agenda is dominated by debates about power; many of the same theoretical and philosophical problems arise that have blocked progress in studying interest groups. Could research on voting have advanced much if researchers had focused heavily on the question of how powerful are individual voters? The issues of the respective power of parliament and the prime minister in Britain have generally been handled better by polemicists than by scholars. A more appropriate approach might have started with the observation that in western political systems, interest groups are a pervasive phenomenon. If we count – as we surely should – organizations such as unions or professional organizations such as the British Medical Association as interest groups, a far higher proportion of the population is incorporated into the political system through interest groups than through membership in political parties. Politicians, civil servants and journalists in all western countries spend a significant (though varying) proportion of their time talking to interest groups. Rather than aiming at the notoriously difficult question of the power of interest groups, political scientists might define as their agenda in studying interest groups the description of group activities, an understanding of why those activities are undertaken, an appreciation of the meaning of group strategies for those at whom they are directed and a comprehension of the meaning of group membership for their adherents. Above all, by taking a comparative perspective, political scientists working on interest groups can demonstrate the modes of integrating interests in society with the state.

Interest Groups in a Comparative Perspective

As anyone who has visited the headquarters of a variety of interest groups will know, interest groups within the same political system differ tremendously in their styles and resources. The Washington offices of large corporations and of what are commonly called public interest groups (i.e., groups committed to objectives such as clean air which in principle, if attained, would benefit the entire public) differ markedly in opulence, atmosphere and location. Not only do corporations have more resources than public interest groups such as Common Cause but the style with which those resources are used is also markedly different. Informality, participatory styles of decisionmaking, earnestness and idealism are more likely to be found in consumer, environmental and women's groups than in business interest groups. Groups which attract members because of their commitment to ideals are likely to find that those members demand a larger say in the running of the interest group than do groups which attract members through promise of a material gain. In brief, interest groups within the same country differ considerably in their structure, style and resources. How do interest groups in different countries compare?

The once popular systems approach to politics may have encouraged us to look for similarities between industrialized democracies in the way in which interests are articulated. In fact, as this book will show, considerable differences exist in the nature of interest groups in different countries. Indeed, as Presthus found in his research in Canada, even the phrase 'interest group' when translated directly into French carries quite different connotations than in English.[21] Interest groups differ internationally in a number of respects.

The first of these differences is the attitude which prevails towards interest groups in the political culture. As Stepan has noted, the differences between English common law traditions and Roman law traditions are considerable.[22] In Britain and the United States, voluntary organizations, such as many interest groups are, have been seen as requiring no permission from the state to form; in Roman law countries (such as Latin American countries), private organizations have generally needed licensing by the state. In some political traditions, *functional representation* (i.e., the representation of citizens in terms of their occupation or economic interest) is regarded as a natural or even desirable event. In other political cultures, functional representation is

[21] Robert Presthus, *Elite Accommodation in Canadian Politics*, Cambridge University Press, Cambridge and New York, 1973.

[22] Alfred Stepan, *State and Society, Peru in Comparative Perspective*, Princeton University Press, Princeton, 1978.

Table 1.1 The density of organization in western democracies; union membership rates in the late 1970s as a percentage of the total workforce

Country	European federation of trade unions' estimate	Unions' own estimate
USA		24.5
Japan		33
West Germany	34–40	39
France	25	23
Great Britain	45–50	50.4
Italy		22
Austria	58	60
Belgium	65–70	70
Denmark	60	70
Norway	55	
Sweden	85	

Sources: Klaus von Beyme, *Challenges to Power: Trade Unions and Industrial Relations in Capitalist Countries*, Sage Publications, London, 1980, pp. 75–6; James Chan-Lee and Helen Sutch, 'Profits and rates of return in OECD countries', OECD Working Paper no. 20, Paris, 1985, table 21

feared or despised as an example of the power of special interests to conspire against the common good. Similar differences exist about the degree to which it is permissible for interest groups to participate in the implementation of public policy. Those who accept functional representation will often see as sensible a devolution to interest groups of responsibility for implementing a policy, an approach which would seem like a betrayal of the public trust to someone critical of functional representation.

A second difference between interest group systems is the degree to which interest groups achieve a high density of membership, i.e., recruit a high proportion of potential members. In some countries, unions recruit nearly 90 per cent of the workforce; in the United States, unions recruit about 18 per cent (see table 1.1). Outside the realm of economic interest groups, however, Americans seem much more likely to join interest groups than their counterparts in other democracies, as observers since

Tocqueville have emphasized.[23] Numerous explanations might be offered for differences in membership density rates, including political culture, the incentives organizations can offer for joining (or punishments they can inflict for refusal to do so) and the role interest groups have achieved in policymaking. We have noted above the important differences in attitudes about the desirability of interest group activity which exist between one country and another. The value of the incentives for membership which interest groups can offer may well vary from one country to another depending on the degree to which alternative sources of 'selective benefits' are available; an interest group offering cheap health insurance in the USA has something more valuable to offer than if an interest group were to offer the same in Sweden. The ability of unions to have workers who refuse to join them sacked varies greatly from country to country, depending in part on the industrial relations laws which prevail. Finally, as we shall see, countries differ dramatically in the degree to which interest groups play a prominent role in policymaking. We may hypothesize that a more prominent role in policymaking for interest groups is a cause as well as a consequence of high membership rates.

A third difference concerns the degree of unity or fragmentation which characterizes interest groups systems. In some countries a single interest group clearly dominates the representation of the interest for which it speaks. The Swedish union federation, the LO, has a practical monopoly on the representation of labour in policymaking. The Japanese business organization, the Keidanren, has enjoyed a similar status with regard to Japanese corporations though there are some signs that this may be changing. In contrast, no one organization in the United States has an unchallenged claim to represent business. The National Association of Manufacturers (NAM), the Chamber of Commerce and the Business Roundtable all vie for the title. A similar contrast may be drawn in the case of agricultural groups. In Britain, the National Farmers' Union has enjoyed almost a monopoly of the right to speak for British farmers; in the United States, four different organizations have

---

[23] See, for example, Norman Nie and Sidney Verba, *Participation in America*, Harper and Row, New York, 1972. This finding is often used by American writers to celebrate the strength of interest groups which in turn are seen as strengthening democracy without reference to the weakness of other forms of interest groups in the USA.

aspired to be regarded as the voice of the farmer – the American Farm Bureau Federation (AFBF), the National Farmers' Union (NFU), the Grange and, at different times, the National Farm Organization (NFO) or the American Agriculture Movement (AAM).

A fourth difference concerns the tactics which interest groups use. The differences in constitutions and political institutions from one country to another produce predictable differences in interest group tactics. Where legislatures and courts are unusually strong, as in the United States, interest groups naturally devote significant resources to trying to work through them. Where the executive is dominant (as in Japan) interest groups use different tactics concentrating on persuading civil servants and ministers to accept their arguments. The opportunities for rewarding individual politicians with campaign contributions in return for a favourable vote on a piece of legislation are greater in systems such as the United States in which party discipline is relatively weak and the autonomy of the individual politician is high. In contrast, in countries with strong political parties, interest groups will often still make campaign contributions but will make them to political parties; the British Labour Party, receiving 90 per cent of its funds from unions, is an obvious example. The British Conservative Party has received a high (though diminishing) proportion of its income from business.

The differences in the institutional focus of interest groups also produce more profound consequences in terms of interest group tactics. When interest groups are obliged to deal with a powerful executive, the most appropriate tactics are to rely on expertise or the assistance that the interest group can give in the implementation of policy. Bureaucracies are more likely to be influenced by technical arguments or by the desirability of obtaining assistance in policy implementation than by the strength of an interest group's campaign organization. Ideally, interest groups which wish to deal with bureaucracies should be capable both of providing useful technical guidance in policy formation and of obtaining a high degree of voluntary compliance from their members with policies to which the interest group agrees. Indeed, as in Japan, interest groups may enhance their status by implementing policy so successfully themselves that the need for direct government action is entirely avoided. Thus, the limitation of the number of Japanese cars which can be exported to Britain is achieved through an agreement between the interest group representing Japanese car makers and its British counterpart, the Society of Motor Manufacturers and Traders; such arrangements in which the Japanese government is not directly involved are common in Japan though not in Britain. In Sweden, incomes policies were operated largely by the LO and the Swedish employers' federation while government remained discreetly in the background. In Austria, the employers' federation has imposed fines on employers paying more than the wage increases agreed with government as part of the country's incomes policy. We often label countries *neocorporatist* in which single interest groups, licensed, recognized or encouraged by the state, enjoy the right to represent their sector of society and which work in partnership with government in both the formulation and implementation of policy sometimes – as in the examples above – acting in place of government. Neocorporatist countries and practices are discussed at length in chapter 4.

In contrast, when executives are weaker, the overtly political tactics of interest groups are more important. Most American interest groups are more obviously involved in politics than their counterparts in countries with strong executives. The selective giving of campaign contributions to friendly legislators, the large scale letter-writing campaign and the mobilization of voters in legislators' districts (grass roots lobbying) are all more characteristic of American interest groups – even those representing business – than they are of interest groups in countries with strong executives.

It is important to reiterate that there are exceptions to all generalizations about interest group behaviour in each country, however. An important reason for this is that, as we noted above, interest groups themselves vary considerably in style and objectives. The National Farmers' Union in Britain, for example, has clearly craved acceptance by government[24] or what Grant

---

[24] Graham K. Wilson, *Special Interests and Policymaking, Agricultural Politics and Policies in Britain and the United States*, John Wiley and Sons, Chichester and London, 1977.

has called 'insider' status.[25] That is, the group wishes to be regarded by the Ministry of Agriculture as a group which has useful expertise, can be trusted to keep confidential information entrusted to it by the Ministry and which will make moderate, not extreme, claims on government. In contrast, the Campaign for Nuclear Disarmament has never aspired to establishing a dialogue with the top officials of the Ministry of Defence; the group has never wanted 'insider' status and has therefore seen no need to change its behaviour in order to become respectable in the eyes of government. A striking contrast exists between two groups in Britain seeking prison reform. The Howard League for Penal Reform seeks a dialogue with the Home Office through 'insider' status, whereas the Rights of the Accused and Prisoners (RAP) has no wish for such respectability.

Yet it remains possible to generalize about the interest group systems of different countries in part because the *types* of interest mobilized differ somewhat from country to country. In Japan and the neocorporatist countries such as Sweden or Austria, the major economic interests such as business and labour dominate the interest group landscape. In contrast, in the United States a far greater range of interest groups are important. 'Citizens'' groups such as Common Cause, women's organizations such as the National Organization for Women, civil rights organizations such as the National Association for the Advancement of Colored People (NAACP) and single issue groups such as the anti-gun control National Rifle Association (NRA) have an importance not matched by non-economic interest groups in other countries.

The Mobilization of Interests

Few issues have concerned students of interest groups more than the question of which interests are mobilized as interest groups, and why. Olson's book, *The Logic of Collective Action*, is probably the most widely cited book on interest groups in print.

---

[25] Wyn Grant, 'Insider group, outsider group, and interest group strategies in Britain', unpublished paper, 1977; Wyn Grant, 'The role of pressure groups', in R. Borthwick and J. Spence (eds.), *British Politics in Perspective*, Leicester University Press, Leicester, 1984.

Olson's contribution was to show that, contrary to the assumption made by pluralists, people with a shared interest did not necessarily mobilize to form an interest group even when they had a reason to do so. Olson's mode of argument was borrowed from micro-economics. Olson's guiding assumption was that individuals were rational, and would not, therefore, expend resources such as money, time or energy unnecessarily. People would not therefore expend resources in pursuit of goods which would be available to them without expending such resources. It followed that people would not expend resources on forming or joining interest groups dedicated to attaining goods available to members and non-members of the interest group alike, irrespective of whether or not they had joined the interest group. This would be true both for interest groups seeking an objective limited to a sector of the population (e.g., farm subsidies) and groups pursuing public goods (e.g., honest government). Farmers will receive subsidies irrespective of whether or not they belong to the National Farmers' Union which campaigns for them. A citizen will benefit from more honest government if such is achieved by Common Cause irrespective of whether or not the citizen belongs to Common Cause. The common sense reply to Olson that 'If everyone acted selfishly like me my interests would not be represented as there would be no one willing to join the interest group' fails, in Olson's view, unless the group in question is very small. The individual citizen, like the individual entrepreneur under conditions of perfect competition, cannot make a decision (e.g., to join an interest group) in the hope that this will encourage others to act similarly because he or she has no reason to suppose that his or her action will in fact affect substantially the behaviour of other citizens. Most of the millions of farmers or citizens will not know of, let alone be influenced by, the decision of a single farmer or citizen to join the NFU or Common Cause.

How, then, are interest groups possible, given that they clearly exist in practice? Olson argues that interest groups are able to exist either because they can compel people to join (e.g., unions in a closed shop) or because they offer selective benefits, i.e., benefits available *only* to members. Such selective benefits are commonly not connected with the major political purpose of the interest group, but are services such as cheaper insurance, tractor tyres, even glossy calendars with pictures of beautiful scenery.

Only if compelled to join or if an interest group offers selective incentives to join is it rational for an individual to join an interest group.

Olson's work has been subjected to a quantity of analysis which perhaps overestimates the importance of his argument to the real world of interest groups. There are obvious objections to Olson's argument. There is a certain circularity to his arguments endemic in the adoption of a mode of thinking used in micro-economics. Thus, if an individual joins an interest group for reasons other than selective incentives, Olson concludes that the person seeks and gains psychic satisfaction from belonging. These satisfactions may well be the reasons which ordinary people might suppose are the reasons for joining an interest group – such as the feeling that one is supporting a good cause or being loyal to one's group. James Wilson[26] and Terry Moe[27] have pointed to the important differences which result for political actions depending on whether the dominant reason for joining the group is the quest for selective incentives, expressing group solidarity, promoting a cause or seeking social contacts.

Yet two points of some significance are still insufficiently stressed in discussions of Olson. First, as we noted above, even in the United States, most interest groups, as Salisbury has noted, are not organizations of the type that Olson discusses, dependent on mobilizing large numbers of individuals, but are organizations such as corporations which exist for some other purpose.[28] It is probable that the importance of organizations which exist primarily for non-political purposes (e.g., unions and corporations which exist primarily for wage bargaining and making profits) is even greater in the interest group systems other than the USA's, or, to use Salisbury's language, that the dominance of institutions in non-American interest group systems is even greater. Writers who would really like to explain the origin and maintenance of interest groups are obliged therefore to think much more widely than did Olson, including in their field of interest not only influences

---

[26] James Q. Wilson, *Political Organizations*, Basic Books, New York, 1974.
[27] Terry Moe, *The Organization of Interests*, University of Chicago Press, Chicago, 1980.
[28] Robert Salisbury, 'Interest representation – the dominance of institutions', *APSR*, 78, 1 (1984), pp. 64–76.

operating on *individuals* but on the factors leading to the political mobilization of such *organizations* as companies and unions which often act as interest groups. A further stage of analysis would be to explain why in different countries and at different times some companies or unions are more active as interest groups than are others. Second, Olson's theories seem to perform poorly in comparative perspective. We have already stressed the differences which exist between the United States and many western European nations in terms of density of membership that economic interest groups achieve. It is highly unlikely that western European economic interest groups achieve this higher density through offering better selective incentives. Indeed, it might be argued that in the United States, which has an incompletely developed welfare state and where individuals are more dependent on their employment contract or voluntary organizations for services such as health insurance supplied by the state in most other countries, selective incentives should achieve a higher density of membership.

The importance of the question why people join different interest groups in different proportions in different countries is however all the more critical because of the inadequacy of Olson's explanations. The fact that we cannot simply explain group membership in terms of selective incentives gives added urgency to the question of why different interests are more or less well organized in different countries. The salience of different issues, the degree to which government have encouraged different interest groups and the differences in group loyalty from country to country are all important explanations for investigation.

It would be churlish, however, to turn away from the mobilization of interests without acknowledging Olson's contribution in raising several questions of enduring importance for the study of interest groups. First, Olson has alerted us to the peculiar difficulties which exist in mobilizing people around interests which affect nearly all of us. Clean air, clean water and safe consumer products are important for everyone. Olson has shown us that creating interest groups to advance such concerns will be very difficult. Even when such interest groups are created, the costs of organizing and recruiting are likely to be very high; the vast majority of appeals to join sent through the post by public interest groups are consigned to the waste basket immediately.

Second, Olson's emphasis on the selective benefits interest groups supply helps explain why members of many interest groups allow extraordinary freedom to their leaders in making policy on public issues; the members of many interest groups have joined not because of the policies of the interest group but because of its selective incentives. Of course, interest groups vary in this respect. As we have noted above, both James Q. Wilson and Terry Moe have explored the implications for the internal politics of interest groups of the degree to which members are attracted by material benefits or by the ideals the interest group pursues. In general, we might expect more vigorous participation in the internal politics of an interest group by its members if it is an interest group which attracts people because of its policy positions rather than its promise of improved material benefits. To the degree that any interest group recruits members by offering selective benefits, its leaders are likely to be free from control by their members, whose interests in their organization are not based on its policies. As we shall see, there are often grounds for believing that interest group leaders pursue policies not supported by their members. Olson has done much to make the internal structure of interest groups more comprehensible.

Interest Groups and Governability

As we have seen earlier, many of the sophisticated studies of interest groups in the 1950s and 1960s suggested that the power of interest groups had been exaggerated. In a sense, these conclusions were comforting. The relative powerlessness of interest groups suggested that the concerns of writers such as Schattschneider, namely, that interest groups might subvert the public interest, were unfounded. Interest groups may be useful in improving public policy by offering useful advice and may enhance the representativeness of the political system by offering an alternative to voting or parties as a means of participation. Interest groups were not, however, a major influence on public policy.

The weaknesses of this research were discussed above. The adequacy of the conception of power used in these studies is dubious. More prosaically, the authors of these studies may well have neglected the degree to which their findings were dependent on the policy area studied, the continuance of what proved to be transient political circumstances (e.g., the rules of procedure of the US Congress) and may have neglected the importance of indirect channels of interest group communication (e.g., through other legislators). Far from people being concerned about excessive interest group power, the question became, as Garson noted, whether or not the study of interest groups had anything to contribute to the study of the distribution of power in society.

The atmosphere changed drastically in the 1970s. In the United States, the country in which many of the studies minimizing the power of interest groups had been undertaken, a new wave of concern about the excessive power of interest groups developed.[29] Journalists were preoccupied with the increasing dependence of politicians on campaign contributions from interest groups. The intervention of single issue groups (i.e., concerned with only one issue) such as anti-abortion rights groups was credited with the defeat of famous liberal senators in the 1978 and 1980 elections and thus with the loss of control of the Senate by the Democrats. Politicians themselves were concerned. President Carter returned from a sojourn in the mountain retreat of Camp David in 1979 to announce that the United States suffered from a crisis of the American spirit (he did not actually use the word 'malaise' by which the speech is remembered) of which one symptom was the excessive influence of interest groups.[30] Somewhat improbably, the Republican leader in the Senate, Robert Dole, lamented the fact that poor and hungry people lacked interest groups to press their case.[31] Established interest such as business increased considerably their interest group activities.

The increase or revival in interest group activity seemed to require an increased attention to interest groups by political scientists. Once again, political scientists started to denounce the consequences of excessive interest group power, not only in the United States but in other democracies. Thus Mancur Olson

[29] For an able survey of the explosion in interest group activity see Jeffrey Berry, *The Interest Group Society*, Little Brown, Boston, 1984.

[30] For the text of Carter's speech, see *Congressional Quarterly Almanac*, C.Q. Press, Washington DC, 1980. Though Carter did not actually use the word 'malaise', the label has stuck as a shorthand and not unfair description of the speech.

[31] Dole's comments are cited in Schlozman and Tierney, *Organized Interests and American Democracy*.

argued that the decline of nations could be explained in terms of the length of time for which, uninterrupted by regime changes, interest groups had been able to steer public policy to their own advantage.[32] Unless disturbed by factors such as war, interest groups would be able to gradually establish patterns of public policy more and more to their advantage, and more and more damaging to the public interest. A group of writers known collectively as the overload theorists argued that democratic governments were besieged by an increasing number of groups pressing their demands on government, demands which government was decreasingly able to meet.

In fact there are a number of different types of overload theorists. Some, such as Anthony King, Richard Rose and B. Guy Peters, have argued that there was a widespread tendency in the 1970s to turn to government for the solution to the problems of everyday life; King gives the example of British citizens seeing it as the responsibility of government to make sure that there were adequate supplies of sugar! Once, King argues, people looked to God to satisfy their needs, then they looked to the market but now people rely on government.[33] Others, such as Finer, have attached more blame to the politicians. Electoral competition, particularly in two party systems in which the rewards for a politician in winning over a small block of voters can be enormous if the group provides the margin of victory, has encouraged politicians to promise interest groups more and more.[34] Finally, neo-marxist writers have argued that although overload occurs, it is due to the needs of the capitalist system, not the demands of ordinary citizens. James O'Connor argues that the falling rate of profit (an assumption common in much marxist analysis) prompts capitalists to transfer more and more of their costs to the state. The costs of maintaining the workforce when its services are not needed through unemployment compensation, the costs of training and education and the costs of research and development are all transferred to the state as capitalists try to maintain

---

[32] Mancur Olson, *The Rise and Decline of Nations, Economic Growth, Stagflation and Social Rigidities*, Yale University Press, New Haven, 1982.

[33] Anthony King (ed.), *Why is Britain Becoming Harder to Govern?*, BBC Books, London, 1976.

[34] S. E. Finer (ed.), *Adversary Politics and Electoral Reform*, Anthony Wigram, London, 1975.

profits.[35] In consequence, *fiscal crisis* occurs. The state grows, but it grows more rapidly than willingness to fund it.

A more subtle version of overload theory rooted in marxist theory emphasizes what neo-marxist writers term a legitimation crisis.[36] The task of the state in capitalist societies is to maintain capitalism through the judicious mixture of restraint and co-option by programmes such as social security which alleviate hardships. Mass consumer society, which in general has benefited capitalists by producing high levels of demand, has also undermined the moral basis of capitalism as people increasingly demand immediate gratification of their interests or demands not only in the marketplace but from the state. The state is of course ultimately unable to meet all these demands and so is unable to legitimate the capitalist system satisfactorily; a legitimation crisis occurs. In consequence, it was questioned whether governments might go bankrupt or whether there was approaching an inevitable fiscal crisis of the state.

The successes of the Reagan and Thatcher governments in the 1980s cast severe doubts on the analyses of the overload theorists. Governments proved to be capable of not merely resisting new demands but of repudiating long established commitments (e.g., to full employment) while prospering politically. Yet even in the 1970s, a different school of writers had pointed to the degree to which, in neocorporatist systems, a partnership between government and major interest groups, especially those representing unions and employers, enhanced rather than diminished governability.[37] There were more alternatives open to societies than merely the choice between domination by interest groups or the total dominance of government. Schmitter, one of the founders of the study of neocorporatist systems, has argued that neocorporatist systems experienced fewer signs of ungovernability in the 1970s than more pluralist systems. Inflation rates and

[35] James O'Connor, *The Fiscal Crisis of the State*, St Martin's Press, New York, 1971.

[36] Jurgen Habermas, *Legitimation Crisis*, tr. Thomas McCarthy, Heinemann, London, 1976.

[37] See, for example, Philippe Schmitter, 'Regime stability and systems of interest intermediation in western Europe and North America', in Suzanne Berger (ed.), *Organizing Interests in Western Europe*, Cambridge University Press, Cambridge and New York, 1981. John Goldthorpe, *Conflict and Stability in Contemporary Capitalism*, Cambridge University Press, Cambridge and New York, 1985.

government budget deficits, for example, were noticeably lower in neocorporatist than more pluralist nations. Economic growth rates tended to be higher. The recovery of the American economy in the mid-1980s – at least in terms of employment and growth – in turn cast doubts on whether neocorporatism was the only way forward. Goldthorpe suggested that neocorporatism and American-style pluralism were equally possible routes to success. Yet the insistence of writers, such as Schmitter, on the positive contribution made by interest groups in neocorporatist systems was a useful reminder that the tendency to assume that powerful interest groups reduced governability was a debatable assumption.

Interest Groups and the State

The role and nature of interest groups depend in part on their relationship to other major institutions, especially parties and the state. The 1980s witnessed an upsurge of interest amongst political scientists in the concept of the state. Non-marxist writers as well as neo-marxists asserted the value of paying attention to the state, a concept which had been labelled as unhelpful and mystifying by American and British writers in the years after the Second World War.

To some degree, the movement to 'bring the state back in' was an extension of the work minimizing the impact of interest groups. Nordlinger and Skocpol, two of the leading 'statist' writers in the USA were both concerned to remind their readers that the state played an independent role in making many decisions and was not merely the tool of societal interests.[38] Skocpol and Nordlinger argued that both marxists and pluralists had erred in emphasizing the degree to which the state was controlled by societal interests. States sometimes acted in alliance with societal interests but for their own reasons; as Nordlinger noted, states also sometimes make decisions without regard to, and even in opposition to, the wishes of groups and institutions in society. Thus the statists can be seen on one level to be joining those who minimize the

[38] Eric Nordlinger, *On the Autonomy of the Democratic State*, Harvard University Press, Cambridge, Mass., 1981. Theda Skocpol, 'Bringing the state back in', in Peter Evans, Dietrich Rueschemeyer and Theda Skocpol (eds), *Bringing the State Back In*, Cambridge University Press, Cambridge and New York, 1985.

importance of studying interest groups.

A different element in statist writings, however, would stress not the weakness of interest groups but the importance of studying the interaction of interests and the state. Pluralists had rightly noted that interest groups make demands upon the state. Neocorporatist writers had stressed instead the degree to which the state uses interest groups not only as a channel of communication but as a means of sharing responsibility for public policy and its implementation with interest groups. Overload theorists, as Birch noted,[39] echoed a traditional interest of marxist writers in the capacity of the state to legitimize existing social arrangements by acceding (on a limited basis) to group demands.

A full appreciation of the relationship between interest groups and the state involves all of these elements. It also requires us to appreciate the role of the state in structuring the interest group system. One of the unique characteristics of the state is that it is both a battleground for contending interests and the structure which shapes those interests. Thus, interest groups seek to bend the power of the state to their purposes, but are also themselves shaped by the state. This shaping takes several forms. Most directly, the state can encourage the creation of interest groups. Examples include the formation of the Confederation of British Industry in Britain in 1964 and the establishment of the Chamber of Commerce, the National Rifle Association and the Farm Bureau in the United States. States also encourage certain types of interest group activity or discourage others. For example, the increased willingness of American courts to accept the standing to sue of interest groups as well as individuals has naturally encouraged American interest groups to devote a larger proportion of their efforts to litigation.

Finally, the structure of the state itself has a profound effect on the nature of interest groups. We have already noted the tendency for governments which control both the legislature and executive (as in Britain) to exist in parallel with relatively united, monopolistic interest groups. This is partly because such governments have both the wish and the capacity to consolidate the expression of interests into a single group so that decision-

---

[39] Anthony Birch, 'Overload, ungovernability and delegitimation', *BJPolS*, 14 (1984), pp. 135–60.

makers are not forced to arbitrate between conflicting demands. (The attempts of British governments to discourage potential rivals to the National Farmers' Union is a good example.) Governments, in systems where authority is divided between different branches of government, are unable to enforce interest group unity by talking to only one interest group; the Executive cannot control which interest groups shall receive a friendly hearing in Congress, or vice versa. It is also the case that those states with powerful executives in control of the legislature are more likely to mobilize interests into forming strong, cohesive groups than are weak, constrained governments. The greater the potential impact of government on an interest, the greater the incentive to organize in order to influence government.

Thus, far from constituting an argument against studying interest groups, statist writings suggest a richer way of thinking about interest groups. Statist writings urge us to look not only at the different ways in which interest groups attempt to influence states but at the various ways in which states influence interest groups.

Interest Groups and Political Parties

It has been commonly argued that there is an inverse relationship between the importance of interest groups and the importance of political parties. Whereas political parties aggregate interests and viewpoints in search of a majority of voters, it is argued, interest groups are by definition concerned with expressing minority viewpoints. Thus, strong political parties have often been seen as an antidote to excessive interest group power.

Such an interpretation of the relationship between interest groups and political parties is simplistic. Strong interest groups can not only coexist with strong political parties but in fact may be allied closely with them. The Social Democrats in Sweden are clearly a strong party, but are in close alliance with an equally strong interest group, the unions' LO. The financial dependence of the British Labour Party on the trade unions has already been noted. In countries such as the United States, with weak political parties, the boundaries between political parties and interest groups can be quite unclear. As Greenstone noted, the Democratic

Party in Detroit *was* the United Auto Workers in many wards; it was the union which provided the money, organization and people to form the party.[40] Similarly, the links between the National Farmers' Union and the nascent Democratic Party of the upper Midwest (e.g., the Dakotas) in the early 1950s were close. Political parties today still act as conduits for campaign contributions from interest groups to individual candidates of the party.

The idea that there is a necessary tension between political parties and interest groups is clearly inaccurate. On the contrary, parties and interest groups in both strong and weak party systems often work closely together. Indeed, an interesting question to ask about interest groups is how they combine links to political parties and other techniques such as lobbying the bureaucracy, which might seem to involve a less partisan, more technocratic approach. The closeness of the links between political parties and interest groups clearly varies from one interest to another. Unions, for example, are frequently more directly linked to political parties than are trade associations representing employers in specific industries. Yet it is probably also the case that the linkages between political parties and interest groups vary from country to country. The links between unions and political parties in the United States are noticeably different (being less permanent and explicit) than are the links between unions and parties in Britain or Sweden. Clearly, there are questions here which we shall have to examine at greater length later.

Conclusions

For all the difficulty of measuring their power in any political system, interest groups remain an important subject for research by political scientists. The concern with the power of interest groups, impossible to measure or even define definitively, has given way to a concern to understand better and explain the different characters and roles of interest groups in the political system.

[40] J. David Greenstone, *Labor in American Politics*, University of Chicago Press, Chicago, 1977.

One of the great advantages of studying interest groups is that they are intermediaries, 'go-betweens' linking government with society and in so doing touching on almost all aspects of the political system. Comparisons of the interest group systems of different countries therefore tell us much about the general characteristics of those political systems. Once we abandon the vain hope of comparing the power of interest groups within a single country or between different countries, interesting questions for research develop. This chapter has described several areas in which research on interest groups occurs and which are suited to comparative analysis. These include the structure and style of interest groups themselves, their relationship with the state and political parties and the tactics which they use to influence policymaking.

The plan of this book has been heavily influenced by the neocorporatist writings of political scientists such as Lehmbruch and Schmitter.[41] As we have seen, the neocorporatists pointed to the fact that in some countries, interest groups enjoyed a monopoly on representing their sector, a monopoly which was licensed or encouraged by the state. Major decisions in neocorporatist countries are made by governments after close consultations approximating to negotiations with major interest groups. Neocorporatist interest group systems clearly differ considerably from those which pluralist writers in the 1950s had in mind. For pluralist writers, interest groups were competitive, not monopolistic, independent of the state not licensed or encouraged by it. Public policy emerged from the interaction of numerous more or less equal interest groups, not from negotiations or consultations between government and a small number of interest groups.

No one would pretend that all interest group systems are as close or as far from the neocorporatist model as each other. There has long been general agreement that the interest group system of the United States is extremely *un*corporatist. As we shall see, the fragmentation and weakness of interest groups in the United

---

[41] Their writings are too extensive to list here in full. Convenient starting points are their edited volumes: Philippe Schmitter and Gerhard Lehmbruch, *Trends Toward Corporatist Intermediation*, Sage Publications, London and Beverly Hills, 1979, and Gerhard Lehmbruch and Philippe Schmitter, *Patterns of Corporatist Policymaking*, Sage Publications, London and Beverly Hills, 1982.

States, which elsewhere form the bedrock of neocorporatism, preclude any other outcome. The British interest group system seems to be somewhat between the American and neocorporatist systems, containing elements in common with each. The interest group systems of France and Japan raise interesting problems in terms of this continuum. Many, but not all, political scientists have argued that neocorporatism exists only where a government, business and labour are involved in co-operative and institutionalized partnership. The weakness of unions in both France and Japan precludes, in this view, calling the interest group systems of those countries neocorporatist. Others have argued that it is the partnership between government and powerful interests which is the hallmark of neocorporatism. The absence of unions from this partnership produces a distinctive form of neocorporatism in France and Japan but, none the less, they retain a form of neocorporatist interest group politics. Without attempting a definitive resolution of this dispute, this book is written on the assumption that there are sufficiently important similarities between the interest group systems of France and Japan on the one hand and the clearly neocorporatist countries on the other to make it possible to consider them together.

Neocorporatist writers not only described existing interest group structures but often suggested that there was a tendency for western democracies to evolve in a neocorporatist direction. Those countries which failed to progress in that direction were likely to pay a significant price in terms of their governability and economic performance. This was 'Still the Century of Corporatism'. Such views have proved harder to defend in the 1980s when neocorporatist arrangements seemed less clearly superior economically than in the past and trends towards neocorporatism seemed to halt. The rapid economic growth rates, low inflation and high growth rates of the American economy in the mid-1980s encouraged those who argued that less neocorporatist economies had greater flexibility and so greater potential for longer term economic growth. The British interest group system, which had seemed headed towards neocorporatism in the 1970s, became emphatically non-neocorporatist in the 1980s. Mrs Thatcher reduced drastically the standing of both the Trades Union Congress and the employers' body, the Confederation of British Industry, in policymaking. The Department of Trade and

Industry was reorganized in a way designed to make neocorporatist links with trade associations less likely. The neocorporatist arrangements of Sweden and the Netherlands, exemplars of neocorporatism, were badly shaken by a variety of factors including economic crisis and declining loyalty to major interest groups. The question became not so much whether neocorporatism was inevitable as whether or not it could survive in its heartlands.

The debate about the inevitability of neocorporatism or the inevitability of its decline need not be settled here. We shall however note the importance of studying the trends in interest group structures over time. Political scientists in the 1950s and 1960s slipped into an ahistorical, static way of viewing the world. The political system was presented as a relatively stable, unchanging phenomenon. In more recent years, political scientists have become aware of the considerable degree of change which has occurred in such elements of the political system as legislative and voting behaviour, parties and executives. The debate about the inevitability of the rise or fall of neocorporatism will remind us that interest groups, like all other aspects of the political system, are not static but are evolving institutions. A proper understanding of interest group systems should pay attention to their past and possible future as well as their present.

2

Interest Groups in the United States

The Ubiquity and Importance of Interest Groups

We have already noted that in 1979, President Carter, beset by political difficulties, retreated to the mountains to ponder his problems at Camp David. The president emerged to announce that the United States suffered from a 'crisis of the American spirit', dubbed by others as a 'malaise', an important element of which was that the political life of the country was too greatly influenced by clamorous, selfish interest groups.[1] President Carter was probably influenced by the difficulties he had encountered in defeating the opposition of interest groups to his policies to end energy shortages, escalating medical costs and to restore the Panama Canal Zone to Panama. In 1987, President Reagan, irritated by the Senate's rejection of his nominee, Robert Bork, to the Supreme Court, demanded that the consideration of his next nominee, Judge Ginsburg, be free from the interest group campaigns mounted by women's and civil rights groups against Bork.[2] Reagan achieved his wish, for revelations that Ginsburg had used illegal drugs forced the withdrawal of his nomination before the interest group campaign, which would otherwise certainly have occurred, could begin.

The occasions on which two presidents inveighed against interest group power were of course occasions after setbacks or defeats which they felt they had suffered at the hands of interest

[1] For the text of Carter's speech, see *Public Papers of the President*, vol. II, Government Printing Office, Washington DC, 1980. Also reprinted in *Congressional Quarterly Almanac*, C.Q. Press, Washington DC, 1980.

[2] *Public Papers of the President*, vol. II, Government Printing Office, Washington DC, 1988.

groups. President Reagan, for example, did not complain about the power of interest groups when his tax cut proposals had triumphed in Congress following strong campaigns by business groups in favour of his plans. Yet the denunciations of interest groups by two recent American presidents remind us about two well-established beliefs about interest groups in American life.

First, there are very few issues indeed in the United States around which interest groups do not coalesce. We have mentioned above issues as diverse as energy, the ratification of the Panama Canal Treaty, medical care costs and the nomination of Supreme Court justices. Interest groups would be found equally active on abortion rights, foreign trade policy, nuclear weapons policy and deliberations about whether or not the birthday of Martin Luther King should be a national holiday. Many outside the United States would be surprised to learn that nearly all the major churches employ lobbyists to represent them on a wide variety of issues, ranging from the tax status of churches to the funding of the food stamp programme.[3] Although there are enormous power differences between different interest groups, it is hard to think of interests – including welfare recipients, whose interests are promoted by churches, unions and organized social workers – which are not represented to some degree within the American interest group system. In addition to such obvious interest groups as those representing business, labour, farmers and enthusiasts for widespread gun ownership (the three-million-strong National Rifle Association), even groups previously thought hard to organize in the past today have *some* representation. Thus, consumers, environmentalists, homosexuals, the elderly and even the poor have some groups which speak on their behalf in Washington, even though it must be emphasized that their resources are generally well below those deployed by the AFL-CIO or numerous business groups. That great observer of early American government, Alexis de Tocqueville, would not be surprised by the ubiquity of interest group politics in the United States today.

Second, the presidents' complaints about excessive interest group power are reminders of the widespread assumption that

---

[3] Alan Hertzke, *Representing God in Washington*, University of Tennessee Press, Knoxville, 1988.

interest groups play an unusually important role in American politics. It has been traditional to emphasize the importance of a number of factors in explaining this. Many have followed Tocqueville in arguing that Americans are more willing than most people to join interest groups. More Americans than any other nationalities claim to be active in interest groups.[4] This claim may reflect the belief of many Americans that they *should* be involved in interest groups more than the proportion who in fact are; the same study showed a much larger proportion claiming that they voted in elections than in fact do. Those who stress the vitality of non-economic interest groups in the USA also often neglect to point out that economic organizations such as unions, or farmers' organizations achieve a lower density of membership (percentage of potential members recruited) than counterparts in other countries. None the less, modern observers, like Tocqueville, can be impressed by the variety and energy of interest groups in the USA.

The power of interest groups within any political system is determined in part by their resources. Interest group power is also determined, however, by the strength or weakness of the other political forces and institutions which they encounter. It has been traditional to suggest that American interest groups face weaker countervailing institutions and forces than do interest groups in other countries. The Constitution, for example, fragments the state into competing, sometimes conflicting, institutions while providing numerous opportunities for interest groups to exert influence by obtaining a leverage point in one or other of the branches of government. Indeed, the designers of the Constitution were very conscious that by constituting the branches of government differently (originally making only the House directly elected) they were making the different branches sympathetic to different interests.

Perhaps most importantly, interest groups in the United States seemed to be relatively unconstrained by factors which in other systems could operate as a severe break on interest group power. Thus, American political parties are notoriously ill-disciplined and weak. Legislators who vote against the party line are subject

---

[4] Gabriel Almond and Sidney Verba, *The Civic Culture, Political Attitudes and Democracy in Five Nations*, Princeton University Press, Princeton, 1963.

to no sanctions, and party leaders fully expect legislators to vote against the party line if they are subject to strong constituency pressure to do so. An important reason for the weakness of political parties is itself another advantage for many interest groups. Ideological differences within the dominant political culture are sufficiently attenuated and complex that many Americans think that their politics are unusually 'pragmatic', whereas of course they are more accurately described as more ideologically uniform than in other countries. The weakness of ideological divisions among Americans creates an advantage for interest groups in that they are able to make an appeal to a wide cross section of politicians. Business groups, for example, find Democrats more sympathetic to their problems than would be the Labour Party in Britain. Class consciousness, in the past a major force in western Europe, has rarely had more than a modest influence in American politics. The supporters of American political parties were originally distinguished by factors such as ethnicity, region or religion to which interest groups could also appeal. It is true that the New Deal produced a re-alignment based partly on class so that thereafter social class has exerted a noticeable effect on voting behaviour in the USA. The impact of social class on voting has been both less strong and less stable in the USA than in many democracies, however. Whereas in some elections (1948, 1964) clear majorities of the working class voted Democratic, in other elections (1956, 1972 and 1984) majorities of working class voters supported the Republicans. The relationship between class and voting in some recent elections is shown in Table 2.1. The weakness of class consciousness could also be expected to allow scope for a variety of interest groups to appeal to enlist the support of citizens whose loyalties had not been pre-empted by class-based organizations. Thus, American interest groups would not be constrained by the usual factors – strong governmental structures, strong political parties or strong ideological and class differences – which restricted their importance in other countries.

For some observers, the alleged power of interest groups in the United States has been a source of inconsistency and unreasonableness in public policy. Lowi's work, *The End of Liberalism*,[5] is a

---

[5] Theodore Lowi, *The End of Liberalism*, 2nd edn, W. W. Norton, New York, 1979.

Table 2.1 Class and party in presidential voting

% of electorate	1980 Republican	1980 Democratic	1980 Independent[a]	1984 Republican	1984 Democratic
26 union household	43	48	6	45	53
15 Income under $12,500	42	51	6	45	53
27 $12,500–$25,000	44	46	8	57	42
21 $25,000–$35,000	53	38	7	59	40
18 $35,000–$50,000	59	32	8	67	32
13 $50,000+	63	26	9	68	31

[a] Former Representative John Anderson.
Source: Michael Nelson (ed.), *The Elections of 1984*, CQ Press, Washington DC, 1985, p. 290.

lament over the damage done to the public interest by the power of different interests over different aspects of policy. For others, the importance of interest groups in the United States has been one of the triumphs of the American political system; the pluralist writers in particular commended interest groups for increasing the opportunities to participate in politics, allowing a wider range of interests and values to find expression, giving minorities with intense concerns an opportunity to override apathetic majorities and above all, dispersing power widely within the political system.[6] Both critics and enthusiasts could agree, however, that interest groups were indeed powerful.

A considerable body of research completed in the 1960s and early 1970s cast doubt, however, on the supposed importance of interest groups in American politics. Two perspectives in this research may be distinguished, namely, those analysing interest groups from an American perspective, and second, those examining American interest groups from a comparative perspective.

The considerable growth in the number of American political scientists engaged in empirical research after the Second World War permitted far more detailed examination of interest groups and the workings of political institutions than had been possible before. Generally, empirical studies suggested that the influence of interest groups had been vastly exaggerated by earlier scholars and commentators. Interest groups were less impressive as organizations than had been supposed, usually struggling to maintain membership and income rather than dominating politicians. Politicians, moreover, were, on closer examination, better able to absorb or deflect pressure than had been supposed. Milbrath's study of Washington lobbyists found that the most successful lobbyists achieved influence not through coercing or threatening politicians with claims that failure to support their group would result in loss of votes or campaign contributions but by being a reliable, courteous source of information for legislators.[7] Lobbyists were in effect unpaid staff for politicians. The studies of legislative

[6] Robert Dahl, *A Preface to Democratic Theory*, University of Chicago Press, Chicago, 1956; Robert Dahl, *Polyarchy; Participation and Opposition*, Yale University Press, New Haven, 1971; Robert Dahl, *Pluralist Democracy in the United States, Conflict and Consent*, Rand McNally, Chicago, 1967.

[7] Lester Milbrath, *The Washington Lobbyists*, Rand McNally, Chicago, 1963.

behaviour conducted by Matthews[8] and Kingdon,[9] though using different research techniques, agreed that interest groups were not a major influence on the voting decisions of Representatives and senators. The extensive study of interest groups in action, conducted by Bauer, Pool and Dexter, also argued that interest groups were uninfluential, in part because they were under-financed, divided, poorly staffed and rarely in contact with any but the friendliest legislators.[10] Bauer et al. went further however in suggesting that even if interest groups were able to increase their own resources, they would still be limited in their ability to coerce legislators. Bauer et al. argued that legislators, representing large, diverse constituencies (even a Representative typically is elected by a district of half a million people) can *choose* which groups or interests to make the basis of their support. On trade issues, for example, a Representative can make either exporters or those threatened by foreign competition part of the core constituency, in effect *choosing* from which interests pressure will come. Bauer et al. argued, therefore, that politicians always had the freedom to form coalitions of interests in their districts congenial to their views. Probably no book did more to establish the view that interest groups in the United States have only limited power.

Work by other political scientists has attested to the value of the contribution of Bauer et al., at least for studying the American political system of the 1950s and 1960s. The link between the percentage of people in a district and the frequency with which the Representative votes in favour of that interest was generally much weaker than had been anticipated; party and ideology were often more important in determining votes on agricultural subsidy legislation than the proportion of people in a district employed in agriculture.[11] Other political scientists have shown that, contrary to the assumptions of Bauer et al., the capacity of

---

[8] Donald Matthews, *US Senators and Their World*, University of North Carolina Press, Chapel Hill, 1960.

[9] John Kingdon, *Congressmen's Voting Decisions*, Harper and Row, New York, 1973.

[10] Raymond Bauer, Ithiel de Sola Pool and Lewis Anthony Dexter, *American Business and Public Policy, The Politics of Foreign Trade*, Atherton Press, New York, 1963.

[11] Graham K. Wilson, *Special Interests and Policymaking, Agricultural Politics and Policies in Britain and the United States*, John Wiley and Sons, Chichester and New York, 1977.

institutions to block interest groups was contingent upon a number of far from permanent features of those institutions, features which might, indeed would, change. In a recent study, Destler has shown how pressure for trade protection in the 1950s and 1960s was absorbed or deflected by a variety of rules and procedures, including the domination of the relevant congressional committees by chairmen electorally safe enough to take responsibility for rejecting the requests and labyrinthine procedures in the Executive branch in which requests for protection from industries could be lost. Only very few, politically strong industries, such as textiles, could fight their way through these blockages while they existed.[12]

A second strand in the revaluation, or rather devaluation, of American interest groups, relied on a comparative perspective. American interest groups in this perspective were not all powerful; on the contrary, they were unimpressive. Economic groups, such as business or farmers' organizations and unions, recruited a smaller proportion of potential members into more numerous, competing or conflicting organizations than did their counterparts in most other industrialized democracies.[13] Unions provide a dramatic but far from unusual example. Whereas over 80 per cent of the workforce of Scandinavian countries is unionized, only around 17 per cent of the American workforce is. Certainly, no economic group entered into the semi-formalized partnership with the state in governance found in the neocorporatist nations. Admittedly, the National Rifle Association (NRA) might be able to block gun control; this seemed unimpressive, however, compared with the ability of the LO to participate in formulating a wide range of major economic and social policies in Sweden. The greatest examples of interest group power would be found in neocorporatist countries, in which the major groups were partners not in governance, and not in the United States, where the most powerful groups, such as the NRA, typically had the power only to block legislation in a narrow policy area.

---

[12] I. M. Destler, *American Trade Politics; System Under Stress*, Institute for International Economics, Washington DC, and the Twentieth Century Fund, New York, 1986, esp. ch. 2.

[13] Graham K. Wilson, 'Why is there no corporatism in the United States?', in Gerhard Lehmbruch and Philippe Schmitter (eds), *Patterns of Corporatist Policymaking*, Sage Publications, London and Beverly Hills, 1982.

By the 1970s, the conventional wisdom of political science was that casual observers or journalists were inclined to over-estimate the power of interest groups in the United States. Too often, however, political scientists forgot that political systems are not as unchanging as many of them in the 1950s and 1960s commonly supposed. In fact, a number of changes were under way in the American political system which had major implications for the power of interest groups. For example, it was possible to argue that interest groups generally had little impact on elections because of the deep loyalty to the Republicans or Democrats which most Americans felt. Most political scientists concluded by the 1980s that the grip of party loyalty on the electorate was much attenuated.[14] Congressional procedures, such as closed committee meetings, the House Rules Committee, the control over committee agendas exercised by the committee chairmen selected through a seniority system which placed in positions of greatest power the most secure legislators and a heavy reliance on voice votes rather than recorded votes on the floor of the House, all played an important role in limiting interest group power. Lobbyists could not monitor legislators in closed committee hearings, the Rules Committee could 'take the heat' for members by refusing to allow a vote on a measure favoured by an interest group and the infrequency of recorded votes compared with the current situation saved legislators from taking a position publicly on a measure on which interest groups were active.

By the late 1970s, most of these supposedly fundamental features of congressional life had changed. Committee chairmen had lost much of their status and many of their powers. In contrast to the recent past, committee chairmen who displeased their colleagues were removed from office by the caucus of the majority Democratic Party. Committee chairmen also lost much of their ability to block legislation because their freedom to control the meetings and agendas of committees was circumscribed by new rules. A proliferation of subcommittees in the House (all, like the offices of legislators themselves, equipped with a vastly expanded staff) showed how control of the political agenda was moving to less senior, and less politically secure legislators.

---

[14] For a balanced discussion of the arguments, see Leon D. Epstein, *Parties in the American Mold*, University of Wisconsin Press, Madison, 1987.

Sunshine laws required committees to meet in public except under exceptional circumstances while more votes were roll call votes as opposed to voice votes.[15] It is true that the Senate showed less institutional change than the House. But the Senate had always been a more egalitarian body than the House; if there had been an 'inner club' of particularly powerful senators in the 1950s, it had disbanded by the late 1960s. The greater competitiveness of Senate than House elections had always made senators more receptive to the claims of constituents or interest groups than Representatives. It is true that Representatives might have been encouraged to assert their independence by the astonishingly high success rate of incumbents seeking re-election (98 per cent in 1986); most legislators acted, however, as though they believed this success rate was due to their skills in anticipating the wishes of constituents rather than the advantages of incumbency as such. In general, though intended to achieve far different results, many of the congressional reforms of the 1970s therefore opened up new opportunities for interest groups.

Perhaps no reform increased the opportunities for interest group activity more than campaign finance reform. Reforms in campaign finance, such as the 1974 Campaign Finance Act as interpreted by the Federal Elections Commission, allowed interest groups to form Political Action Committees which could contribute up to $10,000 to each candidate per election (with up to $5,000 in both the primary and general elections). PACs linked to economic groups, such as corporations or unions, were particularly advantaged by Federal Election Commission rulings which allowed them to pay the often considerable expenses of operating their PACs. Candidates for Congress were eager to raise cash. The costs of running for the House and Senate increased on average by just over 500 per cent between 1974 and 1986 whereas the consumer price index increased by just over 200 per cent in the same period. In the mid-1980s incumbents seeking re-election to the Senate spent on average $3,303, 547[16] so that senators needed

---

[15] For discussions of change in Congress see Thomas Mann and Norman Ornstein, *The New Congress*, American Enterprise Institute, Washington DC, 1979; Lawrence C. Dodd and Bruce I. Oppenheimer, *Congress Reconsidered*, Praeger, New York, 1977.

[16] Norman J. Ornstein (ed.), *Vital Statistics on Congress*, Congressional Quarterly Press, Washington DC, 1987, ch. 3.

Table 2.2 Expenditures by major types of political action committee (in millions of dollars)

Type of PAC	1978	1980	1982	1984	1986
Labour	18.6	25.1	34.8	47.5	58.3
Business[a]	29.0	63.4	85.2	113.2	153.1
Nonconnected/other[b]	19.8	42.6	70.1	106.1	126.9
TOTAL	67.4	131.1	190.1	266.8	338.3

[a] Includes trade associations and groups allied with businesses as well as corporations.
[b] Includes ideological PACs, co-operatives, etc.
Source: Norman J. Ornstein, Thomas E. Mann and Michael J. Malbin, *Vital Statistics on Congress*, Congressional Quarterly, Washington DC, 1987, esp. table 13.7.

to raise on average $2,200 every working day of their six-year term. Of course, some Senate contests were much more expensive than the average. Incumbent senators raise on average 25 per cent of their campaign funds from political action committees; Representatives raise a higher proportion, about 43 per cent. In brief, the political action committees of interest groups have helped politicians meet the increased costs of running for office. PAC expenditures are described in table 2.2.

But PACs are not the only way in which interest group money finds its way into politics. The limit on PAC contributions of $5,000 per candidate per election is so low that increasingly interest groups like to act as 'conduits' for contributions from individuals, who are permitted to contribute $1,000 per candidate per election. More can be given by lobbyists presenting ten cheques for $1,000 from executives of a corporation than by the corporation's PAC. Money can also be given to legislators themselves without breaking the law. The morning of a committee vote on whether to buy its product for the army, a Wisconsin truck manufacturing company invited the members of the Procurement Subcommittee of the House Subcommittee on Defense Appropriations to address briefly a breakfast meeting held by the company in return for 'honoraria' of $2,000. Such 'honoraria' verge on bribery. The extent of corruption as defined by law is unclear. Most textbooks assert that corruption no longer occurs. However, investigations by the FBI, such as the Abscam investigation, in which agents posed as Arabs seeking help with immigration procedures in return for money, regularly uncover corruption in very unexpected quarters; the 1988 trial of Representative Mario Biaggi turned on the ambiguous boundary between corruption and helping constituents obtain defence contracts (who then 'helped' Biaggi). Corruption in American politics is an old story. The creation of PACs, critics charge, has institutionalized it further.

Change in the political system has not been limited to Congress. Other institutions have changed too with implications for interest group power. Changes often mandated by federal courts in the cause of procedural fairness gave interest groups greater opportunities to influence decisionmaking by executive agencies and regulatory commissions and agencies. Regulators were obliged to give interests greater opportunities to shape draft regulations by following more elaborate procedures. Courts became more willing to consider challenges from interest groups, not only to the procedures used by regulators but to the merits of the scientific or economic evidence regulators used to justify their decisions. Even the courts themselves changed important procedural rules in ways which advantaged interest groups, e.g., by providing them with the right to bring civil cases ('standing to sue'), once limited to individuals;[17] in a celebrated, or notorious case, a group of law students were given standing to sue the Interstate Commerce Commission for setting railroad rates at a level which would discourage shipping waste for recycling, the students arguing that failure to recycle rubbish would cause increased use of the natural resources whose beauty they enjoyed at weekends.[18]

The greater openness of American institutions to interest groups coincided with a significant upsurge in the number and range of interest groups. In what Berry has called 'the interest group society'[19] of the 1970s, a wide range of interest groups had developed representing precisely those interests which political

---

[17] For a discussion of these developments, see Karen Orren, 'Standing to sue: interest group conflict in the federal courts', *APSR*, LXX, 3, September 1976, pp. 723–41.

[18] *Students for Regulatory Reform* v. *Interstate Commerce Commission*, 412 US 669 (1973), 689.

[19] Jeffrey Berry, *The Interest Group Society*, Little Brown, Boston, 1984.

scientists had predicted would be the most difficult to organize. 'Good government' was promoted by Common Cause, which after Watergate attained a membership of 400,000, a battery of groups such as Friends of the Earth, the Sierra Club and the older Audubon Society promoted protection of the environment and a number of different interest groups concerned with consumer protection were fostered by Ralph Nader. This upsurge of interest group activity, and its successes in obtaining new regulatory legislation in the early 1970s, prompted economic interests, particularly business, to improve their own interest group representation.[20] By the early 1980s, the United States was once again celebrated as an interest group society whose politics were heavily influenced by interest groups.[21]

What do American Interest Groups do?

In view of the considerable fluctuations which have taken place in the importance attached to interest groups in the USA, it is particularly important to understand the nature of their operations.

In the first place, as the discussion above indicates, interest groups are increasingly involved in electoral politics. Perhaps the first interest group to be involved in electoral politics was business; Mark Hanna, relying on business executives' fear of the populists, raised millions of dollars for the Republicans in the 1896 election. But interest group involvement in elections is not limited to giving money. Interest groups can provide volunteers to work in election campaigns who are sometimes interest group officials on paid leave, equipment such as phone banks to contact and mobilize supporters, propaganda and endorsements. Propaganda and equipment need not be counted as a campaign contribution if they are used to 'communicate' with members of the interest group and their families. This provision of the law allows unions to spend millions of dollars mobilizing union members and

[20] See Graham K. Wilson, *Interest Groups in the United States*, Oxford University Press, Oxford and New York, 1981.
[21] Wilson, *Interest Groups*; Kay Lehman Schlozman and John Tierney, *Organized Interests and American Democracy*, Harper and Row, New York, 1986; Berry, *The Interest Group Society*.

their families to support favoured candidates (usually liberal Democrats) which are not counted as campaign contributions. Endorsements by interest groups are not thought to have much value in delivering the votes of the members of the interest group. But endorsements can help to foster a general image for the candidate. In 1988 both candidates for the presidency, Dukakis and Bush, were eager to be endorsed by police unions to demonstrate their reliability on 'law and order'.

The first interest to become *methodically* involved in electoral politics was labour. By the late 1950s, the AFL-CIO had an important organization, the Committee on Political Education (COPE), raising campaign contributions and systematically distributing them to its political friends. COPE also provided its allies with services such as phone banks, computerized lists of probable supporters from union families and volunteers, including union officials on paid leave of absence, for help in crucial campaigns. COPE also pioneered the systematic evaluation of the voting records of legislators, giving each incumbent a percentage score of correct votes.[22]

In a sense, the history of interest group involvement in electoral politics in the last thirty years is a history of the gradual dispersion of COPE's techniques amongst both economic and non-economic interest groups. Today, most interest groups copy COPE in grading the votes of legislators. Negative as well as positive endorsements are now common; thus, environmental groups have singled out the 'Dirty Dozen' legislators with the worst environmental records. Aided by the 1974 Campaign Finance Act, there has been a tremendous growth in the proportion of economic interest groups with PACs; nearly all unions and trade associations as well as most large corporations today raise money to distribute through PACs to candidates for office. Contributions are limited to $5,000 per election, but clearly 100 interest groups acting in concert can have a substantial impact. There is evidence that certain PACs such the AFL-CIO's COPE or BIPAC (the Business Industry Political Action Committee) trigger contributions from allied PACs when they support a candidate.

---

[22] J. David Greenstone, *Labor in American Politics*, University of Chicago Press, Chicago, 1977; Graham K. Wilson, *Unions in American National Politics*, Macmillan, London and New York, 1979.

Non-economic interest groups, including the 'moral majority' groups campaigning for issues such as making abortion illegal and prayer in schools permissible, are in fact amongst the largest fund raisers for their PACs. But unlike a union or corporation PAC, the independent PACs must pay their operating expenses, which can eat up almost all the money raised through direct mail appeals. None the less, interest group lobbyists generally feel today that every active interest group which wants to be taken seriously in Washington should have a PAC.[23]

Just what interest groups receive for their electoral activities is uncertain. Much recent research has focused on the impact of PAC contributions. The natural assumption to make is that interest groups receive votes from legislators in return for PAC contributions. This is indeed an assumption that has received strong support. However, proof is hard to come by. Legislators naturally advance a host of reasons other than PAC contributions to explain their votes. Their own convictions or ideological predispositions, the interests of their constituents, the arguments of colleagues, party loyalty and even the need to attract the *votes* (as opposed to the *money*) of the interest group's members are common explanations offered. Votes, it is argued, are not purchased by PAC contributions; rather, PAC contributions flow to those whose records appeal to PACs. Indeed, the legislators argue, there are today so many PACs that the legislator can afford to disappoint any given PAC because it is easy to find a different PAC which will make good the $5,000 an irritated PAC might refuse. Indeed, most PAC contributions – even from wealthy groups such as the National Rifle Association – are for far less than the $5,000 maximum. (The NRA typically gives legislators about $2,000.) What then is the point of having a PAC? The traditional answer has always been that a PAC contribution buys *access*; a legislator will not sell his or her vote for $5,000, but will feel obliged to listen to the arguments of the interest group.

This defence of PACs is itself open to objection, however. Can

[23] Larry Sabato, *PAC Power*, W. W. Norton, New York, 1984; Matrick F. Masters and Gerald D. Keim, 'Determinants of PAC participation among large corporations', *Journal of Politics*, vol. 47 pp. 1158–73, 1985; Gary Andres, 'Business involvement in campaign finance, factors influencing the decision to form a PAC', *PS*, (Spring 1985), pp. 213–20.

Americans really be comfortable with the idea that only those with $5,000 to contribute will find access to the political system? Moreover, some careful and complex statistical analyses of the relationship between voting in Congress and levels of PAC contributions suggest that even when all the familiar excuses have been allowed for, there is indeed some relationship between PAC contributions and voting for an interest group's policies.[24] The argument that each PAC can offer only $5,000 per candidate per election though plausible ignores the fact that PACs hunt in packs; a contribution from the AFL-CIO is a signal to all its constituent unions to make a contribution to the candidate. Much the same is true of business organizations. Certain PACs by their own contributions trigger very large contributions indeed. American legislators nowadays devote tremendous efforts to fund raising, with even senators in their first year of a six-year term approaching PACs for contributions. Indeed, it is perhaps somewhat satisfying to note that many PAC officials complain vigorously that they are besieged by importuning politicians seeking campaign contributions. It might also be misleading for political scientists to give PACs a clean bill of health because there is no clear relationship between the votes cast by legislators on the floor of the House or Senate and campaign contributions. Most of the work of Congress is done in committee, not on the floor, and interest groups give heavily to the members of committees most relevant to their work. The pay-off for such contributions might come in the detailed drafting of legislation, or quietly blocking legislation rather than in a recorded vote on the floor of the House or Senate.

Lobbying

It is significant that most studies of lobbying in the United States focus on the relationship between interest groups and the legislature, not, as would be the case in many other systems, on relations between interest groups and the executive which will be discussed shortly. Though this preoccupation with interest groups and the Congress is in part a defect in the political science

[24] For a summary of the research, see Sabato, *PAC Power*, pp. 128–40.

literature on American interest groups, it also reflects the enormous
attention that interest groups give Congress. A recent study found
that practically no interest groups focus exclusively on the
executive branch.[25] While the largest section of interest group
representatives claimed to focus equally on the legislature and
executive, a large minority focused exclusively on Congress.
Labour unions in particular were overwhelmingly concerned with
lobbying Congress, perhaps because of the poor relations between
them and the Reagan administration. In my own study of
the political activities of large companies, their Washington
representatives attached more importance by far to lobbying
Congress than to any other form of action.

Congress is more readily approachable for interest groups
for several reasons. We have already discussed one – PAC
contributions. Senators and Representatives may well also come
from an area where an interest group, though a small proportion
of the national population, accounts for a substantial proportion
of the electorates; farmers are an obvious example. It is probable
that as the American electorate has become more volatile,
legislators are more attentive to smaller and smaller groups in
their constituencies. Moreover, it is customary in Congress for
legislators to seek out assignments to committees which will
enable them to provide useful services to constituents. Thus the
agriculture committees are always dominated by legislators from
rural America and the Armed Services committees contain legislators with numerous defence contractors or military bases in
their districts or states. Finally, legislators generally feel that they
have a duty, as well as an interest in terms of re-election, in
helping interests important to their constituents; Senator Jackson
of Washington was always known as the senator from Boeing
because of his work in securing government orders for the aircraft
company based in Seattle.

It might be supposed that lobbyists should remind politicians

---

[25] Robert Salisbury, John P. Heinz, Edward O. Laumann and Robert L. Nelson, 'Who
works with whom? Patterns of interest group alliance and opposition', Paper presented
to the Annual Meeting of the American Political Science Association, Washington DC,
1986; Edward O. Laumann, John P. Heinz, Robert L. Nelson and Robert Salisbury,
'Organizations in political action: representing interests in national policymaking', Paper
presented at the Annual Meeting of the American Sociological Convention, New York,
1986.

of what the politician stands to lose if he or she fails to accede
to the interest group's demands. As we have noted above, this
has generally been seen as an unwise tactic. There are several
reasons for this. First, it is rarely the case that lobbyists can
guarantee that their interest group's members will actually vote
against a legislator if told to do so. Only a small minority of
interest groups concerned with relatively simple, emotive issues,
such as the moral majority groups or the National Rifle Association, can make the claim with any plausibility. Even PAC
contributions might, as we have seen, be replaced by another
interest group if the lobbyist cancels the group's contribution.
Finally, even today congressional procedures protect members to
some degree from outside pressures; the overwhelming majority
of bills submitted to Congress still die in committee and many
others are crucially rewritten in conference committees composed
of senior legislators from very safe seats.

It has generally been argued therefore that lobbyists should rely
on softer forms of persuasion. The good lobbyist has established
friendly relations with key legislators long before a controversy
erupts. Lobbying itself takes the form of polite presentations of
relevant fact and opinion, and not of attempts to intimidate. The
most effective lobbyist is someone whose opinion the legislator
seeks because it is valuable.

Just how many lobbyists approach this ideal is hard to say.
Certainly the picture that emerged from the study of Bauer et al.
in the late 1950s and early 1960s was of a lobbying profession
which rarely attained such heights. In their study, the average
business representative seemed more of a failed executive than a
skilled persuader. Since then, lobbying in Washington has changed
in a number of respects.

First, the number of lobbyists has increased dramatically. It has
been said that interest group representation is now the third
largest industry of the District of Columbia. The number of trade
associations and individual companies with lobbyists increased
dramatically in the 1970s, perhaps because of the increase in the
number of lobbyists pressing for measures such as stricter
environmental protection which business disliked.[26] Although no

---

[26] David Vogel, 'The power of business in the United States: a reappraisal', *BJPolS*, 13
(1983), pp. 385–408.

one is sure of the exact total, it is thought that there are about 11,000 lobbyists in Washington today.

Second, most commentators believe that the increase in the number of lobbyists has been accompanied by an increase in their sophistication, technical knowledge of issues, and resources. Schlozman and Tierney[27] concluded on the basis of a survey conducted in the 1980s that trade associations no longer displayed the weaknesses emphasized by Bauer et al. Business interest groups seemed well funded, equipped and staffed. It is still possible however to find congressional staffers who take a scathing view of the competence and performance of most lobbyists.

Third, it seems that as the political process in general has become more open, the styles of lobbying are less cosy and limited to Washington than they used to be. A significant number of very varied campaigns involving interest group lobbying have spilt over into aggressive campaigning in the country in general, rather than being confined to discreet conversations in Washington. These include ATT's (American Telephone and Telegraph) massive campaign to be allowed to divest itself of local phone services on conditions it favoured, the campaign against the nomination of Judge Bork to the Supreme Court and the campaigns in favour of President Reagan's proposals to cut taxes and domestic spending in the early 1980s.

Fourth, the vast expansion in the size of Congress's staffs has increased the possibilities for lobbyists to build networks with staffers who handle interest groups' concerns for the legislator. In 1957, there were 2,441 employees of the House and 1,115 of the Senate. In 1985, there were 7,528 employees in the House and 4,097 in the Senate.[28] Although the fastest rate of growth has been in staff employed in the districts or states, there has still been a substantial increase in Washington-based staff. The staffs of the committees of Congress, for example, grew substantially in this period, with House committee staff increasing from 329 to 1,954 and Senate committee staffs increasing from 386 to 1,075.[29] Such large staffs allow every major interest group to have its 'contact person' on the staff of every legislator and

---

[27] Schlozman and Tierney, *Organized Interests*.

[28] Ornstein (ed.), *Vital Statistics on Congress*, table 5.2. [as in table]

[29] Ornstein (ed.), *Vital Statistics on Congress*, table 5.5.

committee. Perhaps the demand for this service is one of the reasons for the growth in staff. Certainly the increase in the size of the White House staff – much publicized after the criminal conduct of members of President Nixon's staff – has been explained in part by demands from interest groups for attention.[30]

Finally, lobbyists employed by interest groups are now joined in substantial numbers by *contract lobbyists*. Contract lobbyists are employed by both specific interest groups (such as corporations) and wider interest groups (such as trade associations) to work on a specific issue because of their expertise or contacts. Contract lobbyists also often serve as the focal point of temporary coalitions working on an issue such as tax reform which is expected to be resolved in a limited time. Of course, there have always been Washington 'insiders' such as Thomas Corcoran or Clark Clifford who turn contacts made during government service into the basis of a lucrative career as a lobbyist. Washington law firms, such as Arnold and Porter, have long served too as lobbyists for their clients. The difference today is that a separate industry of contract lobbying has emerged composed of firms that are not law firms that employ people who do not have the same level of contacts as Corcoran or Clifford.

It is not surprising in view of these developments that many experienced politicians feel that there is more 'pressure' from interest groups than in the past. It must also be borne in mind that even when lobbying seems discreet and low key, a degree of pressure may still be involved. Politically sophisticated lobbyists and politicians do not need to remind each other of the possible consequences for a legislator of voting against an interest group's wishes. Threats do not need to be uttered to be significant.

The best defence for legislators against these threats lies not in the politeness of lobbyists but in the difficulty for lobbyists in carrying out those threats, and as James Madison had predicted, in the multiplicity of groups or 'factions'. In view of the enormous increase which has taken place during the last thirty years in the range of interests effectively represented in Washington, it is more likely than ever that a legislator attacked by one group will find another to protect him or her. Thus legislators were able to pass

[30] John Hart, *The Presidential Branch*, Permagon Press, Oxford and New York, 1987.

a tax 'reform' bill in 1986 which significantly reduced tax allowances for many corporations and richer Americans in part because some corporations believed that the new tax system would be to their advantage. Congress, pressured by different groups both to pass and reject tax reform, was free to make its own decision.[31] The greatest danger of excessive interest group power to the public interest arises not from situations – like the Bork nomination fight – in which the noisy clash of interests is apparent, but in those numerous cases when only one of the interests affected by a policy is mobilized. The silence of such instances frequently masks not disinterested policymaking but the dominance of a single group.

Yet even if the multiplicity of interests involved in lobbying vindicates Madison, in that it prevents a single interest dominating, the multiplicity and fragmentation of interests lobbying also has its costs. Interest groups are often too fragmented to resolve differences within the sectors of society (e.g., business, agriculture or labour), a process known to political scientists as interest aggregation. Moreover, interest groups, usually competing with rivals in their sectors, are less able to pursue the long-term as opposed to short-term interests of their members by being reasonable in their demands. As Olson argues, fragmented, competing interest groups are likely to be more selfish and short sighted interest groups less capable of accepting policies to the advantage of all, including their members in the long term. The increase in the number and variety of groups lobbying in Washington does nothing to increase the responsibility of their demands.

Interest Groups and the Executive Branch

As in all western democracies, the expansion of the size and scope of government over the last century has inevitably led to the devolution to the executive branch of a wide range of responsibilities. Although the Congress has protected its prerogatives better than most legislatures, it is no more possible for

---

[31] Jeffrey H. Birbaum and Alan S. Murray, *Showdown at Gucci Gulch: lawmakers, lobbyists and the unlikely triumph of tax reform*, Random House, New York, 1987.

Congress than for any other legislature to settle through legislation all the details which might arise in implementing its Acts. Details – even crucial details – must be left to executive branch agencies to determine. Interest groups therefore have great need to influence the way in which bureaucrats interpret the mandate they have been given by Congress.[32]

There is no doubt that, as in all political systems, much of the interchange between bureaucrats and interest group officials is concerned with the exchange of technical information and is so technical in nature that it would not be seen by participants as a political relationship. Bureaucrats seek guidance and assistance in implementing policy; interest group officials seek to avoid what they would consider to be ill-informed policy implementation.

The relationship between bureaucrats and interest groups in the United States is unusually suffused with politics, however. The reason for this is that the bureaucracy in the United States is forced by the nature of the American political system to make constant political calculations in its day-to-day work. For the American bureaucracy, apart from having at least as strong inclinations to go its own way as any other bureaucracy, is the servant of at least two, and sometimes three, masters. These are the president, the Congress and the courts. The familiarity of the president's title, chief executive, suggests little more need be said about the ability of the president to issue orders to the bureaucracy. Less familiar is the fact that the committees of Congress which oversee government agencies have substantial power over those agencies because of their ability to reduce or deny agency requests for funds or legislation. Recently a congressional subcommittee displeased with one official in the Agriculture Department went so far as to recommend legislation abolishing his post! Many agency leaders find that the relevant congressional committees are a more vivid presence in their lives than is the presidency, which has little time to devote to overseeing the numerous relatively mundane agencies of government. In turn, as we

---

[32] On this see John Chubb, *Interest Groups and the Bureaucracy*, Stanford University Press, Stanford, 1983; Herbert Kaufman, *The Administrative Behavior of Federal Bureau Chiefs*, Brookings Institution, Washington DC, 1981; Harold Seidman, *Politics, Position and Power*, New York University Press, New York, 1986; Joel Aberbach, Robert Putnam and Bert A. Rockman, *Bureaucrats and Politicians in Western Democracies*, Harvard University Press, Cambridge, Mass., 1981.

have seen, congressional committees are frequently composed of legislators who come from areas vitally affected by the work of the relevant government agency. Thus the agriculture committees are composed overwhelmingly of rural legislators and interior committees of western legislators, from states where the Interior Department owns the vast majority of the land area.

Thus, the agency leader is often obliged to engage in a complex balancing of the wishes of the White House, Congress and interest groups linked to legislators on the relevant committees. Occasionally, particularly in agencies which rarely attract controversy, an 'iron triangle' emerges in which the agency acts to please its attendant interest groups so as to please the relevant congressional committees, whose members in turn are eager to please the interest groups representing their constituents. Although the frequency with which pure iron triangles are found in the executive branch is greatly exaggerated – there are few instances in which congressional committees and interest groups themselves are not too divided to prevent the triangle forming – the concept does remind us that American bureaucrats are not simply administrators. Rather they are political administrators to a degree which, as Aberbach et al. noted,[33] is not true in Europe, attempting to balance political forces which certainly include the interest groups concerned with their departments.

A second unusual feature concerning relations between interest groups and agencies in the United States is the frequency with which the agency takes on a quasi-judicial character. Questions which might seem to involve political choice or judgement to a non-American are frequently subject to quasi-judicial deliberation in the United States. It is amusing to note that a presidential order to the CIA to engage in secret, sometimes violent, actions abroad is called a 'finding'. More mundane examples would include the question of whether or not airlines such as US Air and Piedmont should be allowed to merge, or what the acceptable level of exposure to asbestos in the workplace should be. Indeed, all the regulatory agencies of the federal government are obliged to reach policy decisions by collecting and deliberating over information through quasi-judicial proceedings generally overseen by an administrative law judge. The federal courts have stood

[33] Aberbach, et al., *Bureaucrats and Politicians*.

very ready in recent years to overturn agency decisions which have been made without elaborate quasi-judicial consideration.[34]

The opportunities these proceedings present for interest groups to influence the bureaucracy are obvious and numerous. In the first place, the quasi-judicial process itself provides interest groups with ample opportunity to state their case. The record of hearings on whether the Occupational Safety and Health Administration (OSHA) should promulgate new regulations concerning exposure to carcinogens ran to over 250,000 pages, most of it submitted by interest groups. Second, the cumbersome nature of the proceedings may deter an agency from action vigorously contested by interest groups because the quasi-judicial procedures will absorb so much of the agency's time or resources. Third, even if the agency persists, the quasi-judicial proceedings offer numerous opportunities for delay. The cost of a team of lawyers for an industry threatened with a health regulation expensive to implement may seem negligible to the corporations concerned. The lawyers may be able to spin out the decisionmaking process over many years. Finally, the complexity of the procedures may well allow an appeal challenging the agency's ultimate decision to be made to the federal courts on the grounds that a procedural error was made in arriving at the decision.[35]

It should be noted that apart from the contacts between interest groups and individual agencies, interest groups have also become more closely linked to the White House. Of course, individual interest group leaders in the past have often had access to the president. The AFL-CIO leader, George Meany, was often consulted by President Johnson. Irving Shapiro, leader of the Business Roundtable (a grouping of about 220 major companies) as well as chief executive officer of Du Pont, was frequently consulted by President Carter. But as the presidency itself has been forced to devote greater efforts to mobilizing the public on the president's behalf in order to prevail in Washington ('Going Public' as Kernell calls it),[36] so links between the president and

[34] Richard Stewart, 'The reformation of American administrative law', *Harvard Law Review*, 88, 8 (1975), pp. 1667–1813.

[35] For a lengthier discussion of this argument, see Graham K. Wilson, *The Politics of Safety and Health*, Oxford University Press, Oxford and New York, 1985.

[36] Samuel Kernell, *Going Public, New Strategies of Presidential Leadership*, C.Q. Press, Washington DC, 1984.

interest groups have become more institutionalized.[37] The process began under President Carter with the formation of a unit within the presidency led by Ann Wexler charged with building coalitions in support of the president's policies, a process which involved regular liaison with sympathetic interest groups. The process has been continued (though working with different interests) under President Reagan.

In summary, it would be wrong to assume that contacts between interest groups and bureaucrats in the United States are highly technocratic. On the contrary, such contacts are conducted in a highly political and sometimes even conflictual manner because of the ability the system provides for challenges to the judgement and authority of agencies. When peace reigns, it is because the astute bureaucrat has calculated nicely the relative abilities of all parties to mobilize resources in the White House, Congress and the courts to their own advantage.

Interest Groups and the Courts

A further distinctive feature of American interest groups is the frequency with which they turn to the law. Interest groups reach the courts in a variety of ways. First, interest groups may be direct parties to a civil suit. Unions, for example, may seek an order of *mandamus* ordering an agency to implement an act of Congress concerning occupational safety and health which the agency has failed to implement. Second, interest groups may encourage an individual, who may or may not be a member, to bring a test case, the expenses of which will be borne by the interest group. Third, an interest group may be able, under the legislation creating a regulatory agency, to challenge its decisions in the Appeals Courts. OSHA's regulations may be challenged by any affected interest either on the grounds that its regulation has been made following incomplete or improper procedures or on the grounds that the agency's decisions were not supported by adequate justification on the record. Finally, interest groups may

---

[37] Martha Joynt Kumar and Michael Baruch Grossman, 'The presidency and interest groups', in Michael Nelson (ed.), *The Presidency and the Political System*, C.Q. Press, Washington DC, 1984.

intervene in cases which, in their view, raise crucial issues, even if they are not directly a party to the dispute. An example would be the numerous briefs filed *amicus curiae* ('as a friend of the court') in cases concerning affirmative action (the requirement that federal agencies or federally-funded agencies take steps to see that their contractors, students, etc. have the same proportion of racial minorities or women as the qualified population). Such *amicus* briefs can be seen as a form of lobbying the judiciary. In general, the courts have proved ever readier to provide a forum for interest groups. It is not only that courts have so relaxed the qualifications for 'standing to sue', i.e., bringing a case before the courts, that Karen Orren[38] has concluded that organizations, not individuals, are the typical litigants. It is also that the spirit of judicial activism which gained ground in the United States from the 1950s onwards has made judges happier than ever to resolve major issues. The fact that the courts have been the policymaking institutions on such contentious issues as abortion is well known. It is less widely appreciated that, as Martin Shapiro notes, courts are in practice heavily involved in *economic* issues such as regulation, and have proved ever readier to overturn the determinations of expert regulatory agencies on what constitutes good public policy.[39]

Something of a tradition has developed of regarding use of the courts by interest groups as being particularly advantageous for groups which are incapable of prevailing in other parts of the political system, particularly those groups representing the comparatively weak or powerless. The tradition has arisen because of the fame of cases such as *Brown* v. *The Board of Education of Topeka*, which declared racial segregation unconstitutional, and because of declarations by the court (e.g., in *NAACP* v. *Button*)[40] that the courts have a particular responsibility to listen to the weak. Yet it would be quite incorrect to assume that the courts are used only by civil rights groups. As we have noted above, unions and trade associations bring numerous cases

---

[38] Orren, 'Standing to sue'.
[39] Martin Shapiro, 'The Supreme Court's "return" to economic regulation', *Studies in American Political Development*, vol. 1, Yale University Press, New Haven and London, 1986, pp. 97–123.
[40] *NAACP* v. *Button*, 371 US 415, 1963.

challenging the decisions of the OSHA or Environmental Protection Agency (EPA). Other agencies, such as the Internal Revenue
Service, have to fight it out in court with interest groups whose
members dislike their rulings. Studies suggest that all interest
groups involved in conflict over public policy use the courts,
whatever the character of the group. Moreover, like all other
forms of political action, use of the courts requires resources and
is more readily available to those groups with the necessary
resources at their command. American corporations have never
been short of lawyers, though public interest and civil rights
groups are rarely so fortunate.

None the less, interest groups which might otherwise have
failed have been able to succeed through legal action. Courts have
played an important role in expanding the interest group system
both through supporting requests from groups which at the time
could not command a majority in Congress or support from
the president (e.g., the NAACP (National Association for the
Advancement of Colored People) in 1954) while the courts'
preoccupation with procedural due process in administration has
allowed more groups more opportunity to comment on policy
proposals. Yet the involvement of the courts in so many areas
important to interest groups has also had its costs. In particular,
it can be argued that frequent court cases, inherently adversarial
in character, have failed to promote compromise. On the contrary,
rather than compromise with each other or relevant government
agencies, interest groups may well be obdurate, hoping to gain
in court what they might fail to gain in negotiation. The frequency
of recourse to the courts does something to explain the highly
adversarial character of the American interest group system.

Other Forms of Interest Representation

It is vital to recognize the importance in interest group representation in the United States of people who are not full-time
employees of interest groups. Of particular significance are
Washington lawyers and contract lobbyists to whom we referred
earlier. Washington law firms, such as Arnold and Porter, are
not merely legal practitioners but are also in effect lobbyists. The
size of the Washington bar expanded rapidly in the 1970s, not

because of a growth in litigation but because affluent interests (e.g., corporations) hired lawyers more often to represent them. Similarly, contract, or, as they are humorously termed, 'hired gun', lobbyists are available – such as Charls [sic] Walker – to represent interests (usually corporations) on a specific issue.

When do interests turn to Washington lawyers or political consultants and with what consequences? Law firms and consultants offer help with a narrow issue which might concern a single corporation rather than an entire industry. Consultants in particular also offer a focus for the *ad hoc*, temporary coalition which has become so much a part of the Washington scene, coalitions such as those supporting and those opposing changes in the tax codes in the 1980s which might cut across conventional interest group lines. Finally the 'super lawyers' and consultants offer contacts; they specialize in knowing and having access to decisionmakers who might be inaccessible to an official of an ordinary trade association. A notorious example was one of President Reagan's close associates, Michael Deaver. Deaver left the administration to make money by selling his contacts to interest groups. Trans World Airlines (TWA), for example, paid Deaver $250,000 to make a single telephone call to the Secretary of Transportation. Deaver's other clients were a diverse group, including the government of Canada, which apparently felt that its Embassy was incapable of expressing adequately its views on acid rain caused by pollutants from American electricity-generating stations. Deaver was ultimately convicted of committing perjury when testifying before Congress on his activities. Deaver was not actually sent to jail, unlike another Reagan confidant, Lyn Nofziger, who was convicted of contravening a federal law barring employees of agencies from lobbying their agency within a year of working for the agency. The law was designed to limit the ability of former federal employees to influence their former agencies in return for fees from interest groups.

The contract or 'hired gun' lobbyist is not necessarily corrupt, however. Indeed, congressional committee staffs can find the 'hired gun' consultant particularly reliable. For, to an even greater extent than for the ordinary lobbyist, the 'hired gun' cannot afford to compromise his or her reputation through duplicity or dishonesty in pursuit of short-term gain. If the contract lobbyist deliberately misleads a politician, that politician will never trust him or her again, even if he or she is working for a different client. A short-term advantage obtained dishonestly would result in long-term failure.

General Characteristics of the Interest Group System

So far, we have been concerned with the tactics used by interest groups and their effectiveness. How, though, might we characterize not the tactics of individual interest groups but the nature of the entire interest group system?

The tremendous range of the interest group system has already been emphasized. Interest groups in the United States are today, as Tocqueville found in the 1830s, involved in almost every issue of the day. Nuclear strategic policy, American policy towards individual nations such as Israel, tax policy, energy policy and every other issue of the day attracts the comment of interest groups. Yet, as we have also seen, interest group activity is not synonymous with interest group influence. There are indeed several aspects of the American interest group system which might limit its significance.

First, the American interest group system is fragmented. That is to say, not only do interest groups in different fields compete with each other for influence, but there is also usually competition by interest groups for members from the same sector of society. There is rarely a single interest group which speaks for a sector of society but rather several groups compete for the title. Thus the National Association of Manufacturers (NAM), Chamber of Commerce, and Business Roundtable all make some claims to speak for the business community. The American Farm Bureau Federation (AFBF), National Farmers' Union (NFU), the Grange, and the American Agriculture Movement all make claims to be the voice of the collective interests of American farmers, even though the NFU and AFBF have radically different, conflicting views of what those interests are. Labour is somewhat more united, even though powerful unions such as the United Auto Workers (UAW), United Mineworkers and the Teamsters have spent long periods outside the umbrella organization for labour, the American Federation of Labor–Congress of Industrial Organizations (AFL-CIO), and rejoined in part because of the dramatic

Table 2.3 The decline of labour in the USA

Labour union memberships claimed by unions as a percentage of the total workforce[a]

1975	1980	1982
28.9	23.2	21.9

[a] The figure is higher than in the text because it is based here on the membership as claimed by unions themselves and includes employee associations not generally defined as unions.
Source: Statistical Abstract of the United States, US Department of Commerce, Bureau of the Census, Washington DC, 1988, table 666

decline in the power of organized labour in the USA which is described in table 2.3.

Second, the degree of integration achieved within each interest group sector is limited. The ties between different types of business organization are limited. Trade associations, representing specific industries, are not clearly integrated into the structure of general business organizations representing the collective interests of business as they are in many other systems. Instead, individual corporations affiliate separately to trade associations and business umbrella organizations which may, or may not, co-operate. Similarly, there are dozens of interest groups representing farmers producing individual commodities such as wheat, milk or beef. These commodity organizations have only informal contacts with general agriculture organizations such as the AFBF or NFU. The AFL-CIO has only the most tenuous hold over affiliated unions which reject claims by the organization to influence their industrial or political behaviour. Indeed, the cumbersome title of the organization is itself a reminder of the deep conflict between generally liberal industrial unions (such as the UAW) and conservative craft unions (such as the Carpenters).

Third, American economic interest groups have generally achieved a low density of membership. That is to say, the percentages of farmers joining the farm interest groups or the proportion of workers joining unions is far below the percentages achieved in most other democracies. It is ironic, and important, that, though the United States has been celebrated by many writers as the country whose citizens are the most likely to join interest groups, participation in those groups which would be thought the most obvious groups to join in many other countries, the economic interest groups, are much less successful in recruiting members than their counterparts in other countries. To the extent that the notion that Americans have an unusually high propensity to join interest groups can be sustained at all, it must be sustained with reference to non-economic groups concerned with political or social causes.

Fourth, American interest groups are highly geared to political action rather than more technical activity. Activities such as gathering and distributing campaign contributions, lobbying legislators and, for this too is a political strategy, bringing court cases dominate the work of the American interest groups. Technocrats – economists, scientists, accountants – are employed by American interest groups but the overall atmosphere of American interest groups is more political than in most other political systems. Indeed, it is common to find that economic interest groups advocate policies which seem far removed from their areas of expertise. Thus the AFL-CIO has been the bedrock of liberal coalitions on issues such as civil rights legislation or moves towards national health insurance. The American Farm Bureau Federation has campaigned for issues as far removed from its obvious areas of interest as expelling the United Nations from American soil. The American Medical Association has been accused of forming coalitions with conservative groups such as tobacco interests which are generally associated with products injurious to health. Permanent though informal coalitions or networks link liberal or conservative groups on a wide variety of issues. Clearly, a tricky calculation is required by interest groups. Coalitions have great advantages, broadening the range and number of politicians to whom appeals can be made for support, and transforming what might otherwise seem a selfish interest into something broader and nobler. Yet coalitions can also damage the standing of an interest group by dragging it into commitments which are damaging to its interests or credibility. When the Consumers' Federation was obliged to support protectionist legislation by the United Auto Workers, which had done much to maintain and support the organization in the past, not only the interests of consumers but the credibility of the organization was damaged. The American interest group sometimes seems more like a political party than a highly technocratic, tightly focused lobby for a particular interest. The range of issues on which the AFL-CIO and the American Farm Bureau Federation express themselves is truly extraordinary. The AFBF's commitment for many years to expelling the United Nations from American territory was not exactly closely related to agricultural policy concerns.

Fifth, the interest group system has to compete with a variety of rivals for the title of representing interests in society. Corporations frequently act independently of trade associations or business umbrella organizations, functioning as interest groups in their own right with PACs, Washington offices and lobbyists of their own. Wealthy interests such as corporations frequently turn for help with a problem they have with government to Washington law firms or political consultants, not to interest groups. Most important of all, representatives and senators are expected to help interests in their districts and states in need of help, be they defence contractors, universities or farmers. Frequently, as in the case of the Farm Bureau's claims that farmers prefer a free market to government subsidies, legislators make a judgement of what their constituents want which conflicts with the interest group's judgement. Politicians around the world pay some attention to representing their constituents, regardless of ideology. American legislators, operating in the context of a weak party system, pay unusually great, and possibly increasing, attention to representing constituents' interests. Few American politicians would accept without question claims that a national interest group necessarily represents the views of their constituents for whom it claims to speak. It is by no means unusual for an American legislator to tell an interest group spokesperson that he or she is not speaking for the legislator's constituents.

Sixth, though in practice it is often easy to predict which political party an interest group will favour, ties with political parties are rarely formalized. Thus, though the AFL-CIO has been the most important single source of support for liberal Democratic candidates for Congress, it has no institutionalized place within the party. The AFL-CIO still claims to be non-partisan and the Democratic Party has never set aside any seats at its Convention or on its National Committee for representatives of labour. Indeed, most interest groups, including business, make some effort to avoid being linked too closely to a political party, even while they accept being called liberal or conservative. Indeed, much to the dismay of conservatives, business has given large campaign contributions to those liberal Democrats in Congress who occupy key positions and are certain to be re-elected.

Finally we should re-emphasize the ubiquity and strength of those mass membership interest groups not representing producers. There is no other country in which women's interests are represented by an interest group to match the organizational quality of the National Organization for Women. No other country has produced a 'good government' interest group to match Common Cause. The American environmentalist groups have been rivalled in very few countries (e.g., West Germany). American economic interest groups are unimpressive by international standards. But in no other country do non-economic groups show greater vitality.

In short, the American interest group system, like many other aspects of the American political system, is untidy, competitive, often noisy and very varied. American interest groups play a more obvious role in politics than their counterparts in other countries. It is not clear, however, that their greater visibility is matched by greater importance. In the next section we turn to explaining those influences which have shaped the American interest group system.

Explaining the American Interest Group System

As is always the case, the American interest group system is a product of the state, society and the historical experience within which the system has developed.

The structure of the American state helps to explain many of the features of the interest group system which we have noted. Most obviously, the fragmented American state, designed as a system of separate institutions sharing power and since more fragmented by custom and politics within each institution, provides multiple points of access for interest groups. Interest groups, often each finding a part of government which is attentive, have less need to unite than in more unitary systems of government where points of access to decisionmaking may be limited. Moreover, government, itself divided, cannot enforce tidiness or unity on the interest group system. It has been possible for British governments to require interest groups to merge or to maintain the dominance of a single interest group in its field. The formation of the employers' group the Confederation of British Industry (CBI) and the continuing dominance of the National Farmers' Union are obvious examples. The advantages to government of having a single interest group rather than competing groups will be discussed later. Our concern at present is to emphasize the impossibility of the state creating a less competitive, more integrated interest group system. For even if the White House announced that it would accept only one group as the legitimate representative of farmers, for example, the House, the Senate and the courts may all take a different attitude. Indeed, different departments, or different congressional committees, may respond with differing enthusiasm or hostility to the competing interest groups. The fragmented American state is inherently incapable of promoting a more united, tidier interest group system.

That is not to say that the American state has had no impact on interest groups. Though the prevalent doctrine asserts the autonomy of interest groups so that the Supreme Court has strongly attacked arguments that the state is entitled to alter the balance between competing groups (e.g., by trying to prevent domination of a referendum campaign by the wealthier interests), in reality, the state has often intervened to promote particular groups. The Farm Bureau, the National Rifle Association and the Chamber of Commerce all received useful assistance from government in their early days. It can be argued that industrial unions could not have developed in the USA in the face of determined and often violent employer resistance without the protection of the National Labor Relations Board established during the New Deal. It can also be argued that the decline of unions to their present miserable state has been caused in part by features of labour law adopted in the 1940s. An unintended consequence of the American anti-trust laws has been to inhibit the development of trade associations, so much less important in the United States than in many western democracies. Thus, it is not that the American state has ever lived up to the theory of

Table 2.4 Attitudes towards big business and organized labour in the USA

'I am going to read you a list of institutions in American Society. Please tell me how much confidence you yourself have in each one – a great deal, quite a lot, some, or very little.'

% of respondents saying 'great deal'/'quite a lot'

	1988	1985	1979
Big business	25	31	32
Organized labour	26	28	36

Source: The Gallup Poll, 13 November 1988

leaving interest groups totally autonomous with their development guided only by an invisible hand of competition; state influences on interest groups have been too common for that. However, the inability of the American state to promote a hierarchical system of monopolistic interest groups on the neocorporatist model has always been evident. State involvement has never been sufficiently unified itself to achieve such an objective.

The American interest group system has also been profoundly influenced by the weakness of class consciousness and conflict in the USA. Although American unions once represented 35 per cent of the workforce, the period of union strength was brief (about 1941 to 1961) and was the product of such passing influences as government assistance, wartime labour shortages and the economic dominance of the United States which reduced the competitive forces operating on American employers. The weakness of organized labour in the United States in turn obviated the need for employers to form strong interest groups. The comparative weakness of trade associations and business umbrella groups in the United States reflects the fact that strong challenges to the collective interests of business are rare. When such challenges have emerged (e.g., from unions in the 1930s or from public interest groups in the early 1970s), a rapid strengthening of employers' organizations has been evident. Although a very conservative president dominated American politics in the 1980s, Americans have remained sceptical of both big business and big labour, as table 2.4 shows. However, serious challenges to business have been few. Because of the weakness of unions and employers' organizations, other economic interests – such as farmers – have not been faced with a situation in which it appears that unless they organize, they will be surrounded by better organized interests. In consequence, their interest groups, too, have remained somewhat underdeveloped.

Yet if economic interests have remained weak and divided, non-economic interests have been encouraged by aspects of the American system. The Constitution (in the Bill of Rights) gave interest groups certain clear rights (e.g., to assemble and to petition government). Ever since, the political culture has emphasized the value of participation in non-economic interest groups (while remaining ambivalent about economic, sometimes called *special*, interest groups). The ambivalent feelings of Americans about political parties clearly advantage interest groups. The upsurge of interest in political participation amongst more educated Americans in the 1960s and 1970s coincided with a period of particular distrust of political parties. The public interest groups were beneficiaries of an increased interest in participation which was not directed towards the parties. The comparative weakness of political parties in America has made the money, organization and occasionally the votes which interest groups might offer the more attractive. It is instructive to contrast the political fear which the National Rifle Association instils in the United States with the limited impact of such groups in Great Britain. Interest groups concerned with such foreign policy questions as aid to Israel, support for Greece (against Turkey) and sanctions against South Africa have achieved an importance unmatched in any other democracy. American politicians respond more readily than most to interest group pressures particularly when – as in the case of the foreign policy groups and unlike the situation for business or labour – there is no organized opposition.

Conclusions: Consequences of the Interest Group System

We have argued that the American interest group system is unusually competitive, fragmented and, in the case of economic groups, surprisingly weak. Yet many Americans remain concerned that their system of government is too frequently dominated by special interests at the expense of the public interest. Can these fears be reconciled with evidence that American interest groups are often surprisingly weak?

In fact, they can. In the first place, as we have noted, interests are often represented through institutions other than interest groups. Agricultural subsidies, for example, may be maintained more by the activities of the strategically placed rural legislators on the agriculture committees than by the strength of agricultural interest groups. Similarly, the reluctance of most American politicians to enact more sensible gun control laws may be due more to their fear of losing the votes of the many millions of Americans who like to own guns than to the activities of the National Rifle Association. Support for Israel may be due more to the fear of losing Jewish-American votes in elections in key states than to the activities of the pro-Israel interest groups. American politicians often pursue blocks of voters without any prompting by interest groups. Nor need such behaviour be unprincipled. As we have seen, representatives and senators in the United States often see it as part of their job to advance the interests of interest groups in their districts or states.

Yet, the structure of the interest group system itself may promote irresponsibility. As Olson, amongst others, has noted,[41] interest groups with a wide range of members (e.g., representing nearly all the workforce) can take a more statesmanlike view of things than can less encompassing interest groups (e.g., independent unions representing fragments of the workforce). For the all-encompassing interest group has less need to worry about both losing members to a competitor through showing moderation and seeing its members lose ground if it alone shows moderation while other groups press home their advantage. In brief, when there are numerous competing groups, each group cannot escape the 'prisoner's dilemma' in which though all would benefit from co-operation, none can guarantee that co-operation will occur. It is therefore rational for interest groups to press home their concerns and to forget about making sacrifices to the common good, for they cannot assume that their sacrifices will be matched

---

[41] Mancur Olson, *The Rise and Decline of Nations*, Yale University Press, New Haven, 1982.

by others. Moreover, numerous competing interest groups cannot provide the help in governance that more monopolistic groups can. Competing groups cannot aggregate demands or interests for presentation to government as can monopolistic groups. Neither can they as readily provide assistance in the administration of programmes as groups which are clearly recognized as the sole representatives of their interests. In brief, competitive interest group systems are less likely to assist in promoting good government than more monopolistic systems. The very weakness of competitive interest groups is a root of the problem.

Yet competitive interest group systems can always claim one advantage. The competitive interest group system by definition allows a greater variety of interests to be expressed. A more monopolistic interest group system would almost certainly result in a narrower range of views being articulated with, for example, pro-subsidy farmers suppressing those who wish for a freer market in a single farmers' organization. The American political culture has often placed greater value on representation than effectiveness in government. Perhaps these values are also represented in the interest group system.

Whether or not interest groups in the United States enjoy too much leverage depends not only on them, but on the rest of the political system. As we noted above, the capacity of the American state to absorb or deflect pressure is not constant. Many of the reforms of the 1970s unconsciously reduced the capacity of the American state to withstand pressure from organized interests. It is possible that in the 1980s this capacity has recovered somewhat. Congress proved capable of enacting large scale budget cuts in 1981 and tax 'reform' in 1986 in the face of strong opposition from many interests. Yet any such recovery should not be exaggerated. The budget cuts of 1981 were shaped in such a way as to impose the greatest burdens on those, such as the poor, with the least political power and to avoid interests, such as the elderly or aircraft manufacturers, with strong interest groups. The budget cuts, as David Stockman complained,[42] were crafted to make sufficient concessions to powerful interests to ensure their passage but at enormous cost to the Treasury. Similarly, tax

[42] David Stockman, *The Triumph of Politics, The Inside Story of the Reagan Revolution*, Avon Books, New York, 1987.

'reform' in 1986 was a pill sugared by tax concessions to the wealthy and corporations which had not gained much from the old system. In a sense, the large federal budget deficit is a reminder of how important interest groups have become in the 1970s and 1980s. Whether the United States can continue to afford to allow such success to fragmented, selfish interest groups remains to be seen.

3

The British Interest Group System

One of the major attractions for some and frustrations for others of the British interest group system is the contrasts and contradictions it contains. Viewed from one angle, British interest groups, like American interest groups, are fragmented and competing groups are kept quite distinct from government. Trade associations in particular are much weaker and less important than their counterparts in many other European countries, such as West Germany. Viewed from another angle, Britain displays more in common with the neocorporatist countries with interest groups such as the National Farmers' Union (NFU) enjoying a virtual monopoly of representation in its sector and closely integrated with its sponsoring ministry, the Ministry of Agriculture, Fisheries and Food (MAFF). The density of membership achieved by economic interest groups may seem high by American standards (with unions organizing 48 per cent of the workforce as opposed to 17 per cent in the USA), but would seem puny by Scandinavian standards (where over 80 per cent of the workforce is organized). The close partnership between the NFU and MAFF or between trade associations and the Department of Trade and Industry would seem too close for comfort to many American observers in the public interest group tradition of distrusting links between 'special interests' and government. Government and major economic interests would seem dangerously remote from each other to observers from neocorporatist countries, or France and Japan, who would emphasize the absence of institutionalized partnerships between government and interest groups in the making of general economic or industrial policy. It is amusing to note that while political scientists interested in neocorporatism have ranked Britain very low on scales of neocorporatism, the

Table 3.1 Attitudes towards the role of interest groups in policymaking in Britain

'*When governments make decisions about the economy, which is better – to involve major interests like trade unions and business or to keep them at arm's length?*

	1986	1985
Involve	68	69
Keep at arm's length	23	22
Don't know/neither/both	9	9

Source: SSLT (Gallup), 1986

Thatcher government has attributed British economic problems in the 1970s to an excess of neocorporatism.[1]

Disagreements among commentators about the importance of British interest groups in political life have been accompanied by a similar uncertainty about interest groups in normative discussions. The British are ambivalent about the role that interest groups *ought* to play in their politics. As we noted in chapter 1, some elements in the British political culture welcome interest group activity on the grounds that functional representation (i.e., representation on the basis of one's economic role) is a valuable supplement or alternative to geographic representation. Table 3.1 presents some interesting data on attitudes towards the role of interest groups in policymaking in Britain. Both older, pre-Thatcher forms of paternalistic Conservativism and the Labour Party's association with the trade unions encourage an acceptance of a prominent role for economic interest groups in policymaking. Paternalistic Conservativism's vision of society as a harmonious

---

[1] For an example of a scale of neocorporatism which puts Britain very low down the scale see Philippe Schmitter, 'Interest intermediation and regime governability in contemporary western Europe and North America', in Suzanne Berger (ed.), *Organizing Interests in Western Europe*, Cambridge University Press, Cambridge, 1981. For the Thatcher government's criticisms of corporatism as contributing to Britain's decline – and attempts to break up the corporatist links of the Department of Trade and Industry – see Department of Trade and Industry, *DTI – The Department for Enterprise* Cmnd 278, HMSO, London, 1988. For a history of moves towards and away from neocorporatism since the First World War, see R. K. Middlemass, *The Politics of Industrial Society: The Experience of British Society Since 1911*, Andre Deutsch, London, 1979.

organic whole predisposed its adherents to consult those interests which constitute society. The Labour Party's links to unions inclined it to involve unions in policymaking; other interests could not be denied similar opportunities. Yet British culture also contains elements very hostile to neocorporatism. Liberal strands in British culture fear collusion between government and interest groups. The traditional supremacy of parliament seems threatened if interest groups become more important than elected politicians. Arguments that Britain had become neocorporatist in the 1970s were seen as cause for alarm in a way which would not be true in Austria or Sweden.

Although the normative debate in Britain about the role of interest groups goes back at least to before the Second World War and writers such as Laski, the importance of interest groups in British government has been acknowledged only since the 1960s[2] and is still overshadowed in the minds of many observers by such features of the political system as tightly disciplined political parties. Indeed, it is easy to see why it used to be thought that interest groups would inevitably play a much smaller role in the British than in the American political system. British voters used to be thought to be too tied by class and party loyalties to political parties to be susceptible to appeals from interest groups to change their vote.[3] British political parties, tightly controlled in the House of Commons, would provide no scope for interest groups to defeat government legislation by mobilizing sympathetic legislators. Nor would parliament have enough independence to provide a power base which interest groups could use, as in American iron triangles, to pull government agencies away from allegiance to central policy and towards their own concerns. British courts, constitutionally incapable of nullifying an Act of Parliament and generally unwilling to challenge the executive,

[2] For pioneering works on British interest groups, see: Samuel Finer, *Anonymous Empire*, Pall Mall Press, London 1966; Harry Eckstein, *Pressure Politics, The Case of the BMA*, University of California Press, Berkeley, 1963; Peter Self and Herbert Storing, *The State and the Farmer*, Allen and Unwin, London, 1962 and 1971.

[3] David Butler and Donald Stokes, *Political Change in Britain*, 2nd edn, Macmillan, London, 1974. Peter Pulzer was the author of the aphorism that class is everything in explaining voting behaviour in Britain; all else is embellishment. Peter Pulzer, *Political Representation and Elections in Britain*, Allen and Unwin, London, 1967, p. 96. For an excellent review of the decline of class voting, see Richard Rose and Ian McAllister, *Voters Begin To Choose*, Sage Publications, Beverly Hills, 1986.

provide few opportunities to interest groups comparable to the American courts. Indeed, one might ask what do British interest groups actually do given the limitations under which they operate?

The Activities of British Interest Groups

It must be admitted at the outset that British government is not nearly as impervious to outside pressures as the account above suggests. Indeed, as we shall discuss later, it was fashionable in the late 1970s to suggest that British interest groups were clearly overly powerful *vis-à-vis* government which was overloaded by interest group demands it could not meet.[4] MPs are not as much the domesticated poodles that our discussion above suggests as they are well-trained dogs that occasionally, however, slip the leash. MPs have been increasingly willing to abstain or even vote against their party leaders.[5] Moreover, the less dramatic forms of action MPs can take, such as asking parliamentary questions, exerting pressure on ministers at meetings of the backbenchers' committees, lobbying ministers informally and exerting pressure through the select committees of parliament, make MPs more useful for interest groups than one might think. Indeed, one of the faster growing occupations in the 1980s was the *contract lobbyist* working on a retainer like the Washington political consultant for those interests desiring his or her services. We shall discuss this development further below.

MPs are nearly always ready to meet interest group representatives. Interest groups are potentially a source of information for MPs who have to operate without the benefit of staffs in any way comparable to those of American legislators. Whatever their weaknesses as a form of objective analysis, information or arguments supplied by interest groups provide MPs with some information; MPs do not have the resources to generate much information themselves. Nor is it the case that MPs behave as though loyalty to the party alone determines their ability to win re-election. Even though the electoral reward for being an MP

[4] Anthony King (ed.), *Why is Britain Becoming Harder to Govern?*, BBC Publications, London, 1976; Richard Rose and B. Guy Peters, *Can Governments Go Bankrupt?*, Basic Books, New York, 1978.

[5] Philip Norton, *Dissension in the House of Commons*, Macmillan, London, 1975.

who takes good care of the constituency is less than in the USA, votes going to the person, not the party, keep a significant number of MPs in their jobs.[6] It is possible that, though on a more modest scale than in the USA, there is in Britain an 'incumbency effect' so that good constituency MPs are able to withstand a swing against their party which should result in their defeat. Moreover, most MPs see representing interests in their constituencies as part of the job. Indeed, many MPs have a formalized relationship with an interest group which would be regarded as scandalous in the USA. That is to say, many backbench MPs receive a salary, or as it is called, a retainer, from interest groups on the understanding that they will give advice and assistance to the interest group on issues which concern it. Although MPs on such retainers are expected to 'declare an interest' if they speak on behalf of an interest group's cause, there are few other restrictions on this widespread practice. Many members of the House of Lords, particularly the ever more dominant life peers, have been given peerages precisely because of their links to interest groups. The ennobled former union leader as well as former industrialist are frequent participants in House of Lords debates.

Yet few would deny that links between interest groups and MPs are generally seen as a useful supplement to major activities, an indirect way of putting across the interest group's cause to those really in power. In the British context, those really in power are to be found in the executive branch of government. For, notwithstanding the increase in the number of backbenchers' rebellions which Norton has documented, the vast majority of government Bills clear parliament without substantial amendment. Once policy is presented to parliament, the policy is likely to prevail. Relatively little will be done to change it. It follows that the most important decisions for interest groups to influence are inside the 'black box' of decisionmaking which takes place between ministers and civil servants, veiled from public scrutiny by the doctrines of secrecy that characterize British government.

Fortunately for interest groups, it is often easy for them to participate in this policymaking process from which the general

---

[6] Bruce Cain, John Ferejohn and Maurice Fiorina, 'The constituency service basis of the personal vote for US representatives and British members of parliament', *APSR*, 78, 1 (March 1984), pp. 10–125.

public is excluded. Government departments, though only rarely under a statutory obligation to consult interest groups (agriculture being an important exception), generally feel that policy should be prepared after close consultation with affected interests. Indeed, the officials of interest groups closely consulted by government departments are frequently on first-name terms with their civil service counterparts. Consultations take many forms. Formal meetings with government agencies at which analyses of policy proposals are presented and defended are not the only form of contact between interest groups and ministries. On the contrary, regular, sometimes daily, exchanges between interest group officials, civil servants and ministers take place by phone, over lunch or in London clubs. Commentators who have emphasized the absence of institutionalized forms of consultation in Britain, without noting the prevalence of informal consultations between government and interest groups, present an incomplete picture of the relationship.

Why do British government agencies consult interest groups so frequently? The formative studies of interest groups in Britain identified several administrative advantages for government in working closely with interest groups.

First, interest groups provide advice. It is frequently overlooked that, even today, the British government possesses little technical knowledge or expertise. For British central government traditionally administers directly very few activities, though power has been centralized considerably by the Thatcher governments. At least since Tudor times, the British state has devolved the administration of its policies to subordinate organizations, first to justices of the peace and later to local government, which today administers such services as education or road maintenance on behalf of central government. Even nationalized industries have been run through appointed boards offering much theoretical and some practical insulation from the sponsoring government department. Government departments are not supposed to involve themselves in the detailed management of nationalized industries for which they are responsible, though in practice interference on politically sensitive questions is commonplace. Further, the British civil service has always preferred the 'generalist' administrator who, with a liberal arts education, moves from ministry to ministry over the technical specialist with a scientific or technical education who remains in the same policy area. Generalists are more likely to occupy the top positions than officials from technical branches of the civil service. British governments, in short, have not had the resources to evaluate fully for themselves policy proposals. Even if greater centralization of control over local government, universities and education under the Thatcher governments has changed the position somewhat, the long history of a lack of expertise in central government itself has produced an administrative culture in which consulting interest groups in order to obtain technical advice is as natural as drinking tea. Civil servants instinctively look to interest groups to help fill the gaps which traditionally existed in the information available to governments.

Second, interest groups give legitimacy to government policies which they approve. As Beer noted,[7] the British political culture has long recognized the virtues of functional representation – representation through occupational or economic groups. The assurance that 'all interested parties have been consulted and have indicated their approval' can smooth a policy's progress through parliament. Interest group approval has, therefore, a certain political value for governments and in some cases, such as negotiations between the National Farmers' Union and the Ministry of Agriculture, governments have been prepared to pay (through increased farm subsidies) for the approval of interest groups. Conversely, though interest groups are unable to defeat government proposals in parliament, they are able to mount campaigns in and out of parliament which may embarrass and even damage the government through presenting it as obdurate, stupid or ill advised.

Third, interest groups help in policy implementation. The National Farmers' Union was long entrusted with the implementation of policies aimed at promoting good farming practices.[8] British governments have been able to devolve the difficult choices on occupational safety and health policy to a body, the Health and Safety Commission (HSC), which is dominated by representatives of employers and unions.[9] Wide areas of regulation in Britain

[7] Samuel Beer, *Modern British Politics*, Faber and Faber, London, 1965.
[8] Self and Storing, *The State and the Farmer*.
[9] Graham K. Wilson, *The Politics of Safety and Health*, Oxford University Press, Oxford and New York, 1985.

involve 'self regulation' in which the regulated interest itself accepts responsibility for securing safe practices. Comparative studies of regulation suggest that self regulation has achieved at least as much as, and probably more than, more legalistic forms of regulation by government in the United States.[10] The continuing faith in self regulation in Britain is evident in the financial sector, where the Stock Exchange is given responsibilities for ensuring honesty which in the United States are given to a government agency, the Securities and Exchange Commission.

In addition to these administrative reasons for consulting interest groups, British governments have had to accept that certain interests in society have great abilities to disrupt their plans or society. Until Mrs Thatcher reduced their power, both Conservative and Labour governments feared the disruption which unions could cause. The devastation inflicted on Britain's economy and society by the coal miners in 1973 and 1974 demonstrated why prime ministers had pleaded with union leaders over beer and sandwiches at No. 10 Downing Street for union acceptance of their policies. Usually less dramatic, but at least as important, is the possibility that investment capital can flee overseas if British government policies are seen as damaging to capital.[11] Indeed, any future Labour government in Britain would have to realize that modern finance markets linked electronically round the world could produce a massive flight of capital from Britain if policies were seen as a threat to capital. A Labour government might need friendly relations with business organizations more than would a Conservative government in order to provide reassurance to investors. Discussions with interest groups which can avoid economically or socially damaging action by powerful interests are clearly valuable for government.[12]

Finally, it must be remembered that the government departments consulting interest groups retain considerable control over the relationship. The promise to consult interest groups, for example,

---

[10] David Vogel, *National Styles of Regulation*, Cornell University Press, Ithaca, 1986.
[11] David Marsh and Gareth Locksley, 'Capital in Britain; its structural power and influence over policy', *Western European Politics*, 6, 2 (April 1983), pp. 36–60.
[12] For a most useful discussion of whether or not the tradition of extensive consultation by government with interest groups in Britain is much the same thing as neocorporatism, see Grant Jordan and J. J. Richardson, *Government and Pressure Groups in Britain*, Oxford University Press, Oxford, 1987.

can be implemented in a variety of ways which give the interest group real or limited opportunities to influence government. Consultation for favoured groups will be constant, close, detailed, and, most important of all, will take place in confidence at an early stage of policy development so that government will not be embarrassed by changing its mind. In contrast, a less favoured group will be allowed to make a formal presentation to politely attentive civil servants or junior ministers who know full well that nothing the group says will influence them. Most valuable of all for civil servants and ministers, an interest group can be moved along the spectrum of consultation which ranges from close, effective consultation to the merely formal, according to the current attitude of the ministry to the group in question. Thus a group which is perceived to be acting irresponsibly or making 'unreasonable' demands can have its opportunities for influencing policymakers downgraded towards the merely formal. A group prepared to act more responsibly or reasonably may find its opportunities for influencing policymakers upgraded.

British interest groups, as we have emphasized, think mainly of trying to influence the executive. Very frequently the whole style and structure of the interest groups echo that of the government departments on which they focus. Many interest group officials look, talk and write just like the civil servants with whom they spend so much time. Thus, in contrast with American interest groups, the British are more technocratic, less political and have been traditionally less likely to use the courts. This is not to say that British interest groups have avoided the courts entirely; unions in particular fight numerous injury cases on behalf of their members. Moreover, there seems to be a trend for interest groups to use the courts more than in the past to pursue general policy goals, perhaps because judges seem somewhat more willing to consider challenges to the way in which ministers have used or interpreted legislation, as when Sir Freddie Laker was able to gain rights to offer low price flights across the Atlantic through legal action.

It may well be that this trend for interest groups to take legal action to further their policies will continue. If British judges are more willing to challenge ministers than in the past, the strategy will be increasingly attractive. Moreover, the denationalization of major industries in Britain, because it is accompanied by the

creation of regulatory bodies such as the Office of Telecommuni-
cations, will almost certainly lead, as in the USA, to major issues
between the regulators, the industry in question and consumer
groups being settled in court. Affected interests will seek to use
legal arguments to advance their cause. Another interesting
development to watch, however, will be whether British interest
groups are able to make increased use of European courts which
show less deference to the executive than do British courts. Britain
is committed through treaty to allow the submission of cases to
a number of different European courts. Economic issues may
reach the European Court, an institution of the European
Community. The decisions of the court can be enforced by
the Commission of the European Court. A more voluntary
commitment is to accept the decisions of the European Court of
Human Rights, the court which hears cases alleging non-
compliance with the provisions of the European Convention on
Human Rights, to which Britain is a signatory. There are no
mechanisms to enforce compliance with the court's decisions,
which, however, Britain has honoured because it wishes to comply
with its treaty obligations. In both cases, recourse to the British
courts must be exhausted before the case can be considered by
European courts.

The future may see British interest groups use courts much
more frequently than in the past. However, so far courts are used
much less frequently by interest groups in Britain than in the
USA. Moreover, fundamental features of the British constitution
will continue to constrain use of the courts. Parliamentary
sovereignty ensures that any decision of a British court can be
reversed by a new Act of Parliament. European courts are in a
somewhat different position, as their authority is derived from
treaties which Britain alone cannot change. But relatively few
cases reach the European courts, and so far British judges have
not been as willing as their American counterparts to overrule
the decisions of the executive or legislature.

Most British interest groups avoid links with political parties.
A few do not. The risk of being associated with a particular
political party is that the interest group will have little influence
when the political party with which it is not associated is in
power. The CBI and the NFU are eager not to be associated with
the Conservatives, even if their members vote Conservative, in

order to have some credibility with Labour governments. Yet some large companies, particularly in the brewing and construction industries, have been closely associated with the Conservative Party. Though perhaps as few as 10 per cent of large companies in Britain give to the Conservative Party, companies account for about half the party's income, a significant if diminishing proportion. (The Conservative Party has been trying to move towards greater reliance on individual contributors.) In the early 1980s, a most interesting conflict broke out between business executives who wanted to criticize policies of the Thatcher government such as high interest rates and a high exchange rate for the pound which, designed to reduce inflation, had the effect of increasing business bankruptcies drastically. After the head of the CBI threatened the government with 'a bare knuckle fight' unless policies less damaging to business were adopted, business executives who were strong Conservative supporters withdrew, or threatened to withdraw, their companies from the CBI. The director-general of the CBI retreated, though Grant argues that the CBI's influence never fully recovered.[13] Non-partisanship had its limits.

The unions constitute the greatest exception to the strategy of non-partisanship favoured by most interest groups. Unions provide over 90 per cent of the funds of the Labour Party and cast 'block votes' at the Labour Party Conference equal to over 80 per cent of all votes cast. The block votes are supposedly equivalent to the number of people in each union who have joined the Labour Party through the union. However, many people who belong to the Labour Party through their union are unaware of the fact; they have simply failed to complete the form which would allow them not to be a member, a process known as 'contracting out'. It is amusing to watch union leaders cast millions of votes at the Labour Party Conference supposedly on behalf of their members without showing any recognition of the fact that nearly a third of their members voted Conservative in the General Election, and that most union members did not vote Labour. Under the new system for selecting the leader of the Labour Party in the House of Commons – who would become prime minister if there were another Labour government – unions have 40 per cent of the

---

[13] Grant, 'Insider groups, outsider groups', (unpublished paper).

Table 3.2 Attitudes towards unions in Britain

'Generally speaking, and thinking of Britain as a whole, do you think that unions are a good thing or a bad thing?'

% of respondents replying

	Good thing	Bad thing	Don't know
1986	67	22	11
1976	56	28	16
1971	62	21	17
1966	63	20	17
1961	57	27	16
1956	61	20	19

Source: SSLT (Gallup), 1986

votes in the Electoral College that makes the decision, a larger proportion than that given to either the parliamentary Labour Party or the constituency Labour Parties. The deputy leader of the Labour Party in the House of Commons is selected in the same way.

The reasons for the unions' close ties to the Labour Party are partly historical. The Labour Party, as the great union leader and Labour Party politician, Ernest Bevin, once remarked graphically, sprang from the bowels of the unions. The Labour Party is still to this day dependent on the unions, as we have seen. The unions' close links to the Labour Party also reflect, however, an ambivalence in the minds of union leaders about whether they are leaders of interest groups improving the wages and conditions of their members or whether they are part of a labour *movement* which has as its ultimate objective the transformation of society.

The main constraints on the power of unions within the Labour Party have been the unpopularity of unions and divisions between unions. Although as Table 3.2 shows British public opinion is in general strongly in favour of the right to join a union, public opinion – as Table 3.3 shows – since the Second World War has also been very critical of the activities and, according to many, the excessive power of union leaders. Until the Thatcher reforms in labour law were adopted, even most union members thought that unions had too much power. In consequence, Labour leaders

Table 3.3 Attitudes towards the power of unions in Britain

'Do you think trade unions are becoming too powerful, are not powerful enough or are about right?'

	% of respondents replying	
	1986	1985
Too powerful	45	53
Not powerful enough	13	12
About right	36	29
Don't know	6	6

Source: SSLT (Gallup), 1986

can be hurt electorally by close association with union leaders. The divisions among union leaders on many public policy questions – one union leader is even against unilateral nuclear disarmament in the hope that France, China, Israel, the Soviet Union, Pakistan, India and South Africa will follow suit – also give the rest of the Labour Party some leverage. The internal politics of unions are arcane and confusing. Inspite of the importance of their role in the Labour Party we have little sense, therefore, of what makes the leadership of a union left or right wing. The Transport and General Workers' Union shifted from being led by the right (in Labour Party terms) to being lead by the left in the 1950s; this change, which has arguably ever since had a profound effect not only on the politics of the Labour Party but through it on the country in general, is little understood. Power struggles in the Transport and General Workers' Union are about as easily followed by the general public or its members as are power struggles in the Kremlin.

None the less, shifts in the political balance between the left and the right in unions have had important consequences for the Labour Party and therefore British politics in general. Up to the late 1950s, the role of the unions on balance was to help leaders of the parliamentary Labour Party fight off pressure from the left dominated constituency parties. Union leaders were rarely much interested in politics, and tended to be on the right of the party when they were. Although important shifts to the left were apparent in the 1950s, notably with the drastic change in the position of the Transport and General Workers' Union noted above, events in the 1960s and 1970s politicized and radicalized union leaders further. Both Labour and Conservative governments identified industrial relations as an important cause of Britain's economic decline and attempted to change union behaviour through legislation. Both Labour and Conservative governments operated statutory incomes policies, 'interfering' in the fundamental activity of a union, namely, wage bargaining. The union leaders found their most fervent supporters in opposition to these policies on the left of the party, and the alliance of the Labour left and the unions culminated in the removal of the right to choose its leader from the parliamentary Labour Party in 1981. Ultimately an increased awareness of the consequences of the policies of the Thatcher government for unions – membership, legal powers and political influence all declining markedly during Mrs Thatcher's prime ministership – prompted a 'new realism' among some previously left-wing union leaders, who realized the need to shift the Labour Party back towards the political centre if it were ever to form a government again. Unfortunately for Labour Party leaders, this change of heart was not complete (particularly on defence policy) and was accompanied by demands from the unions for repeal of popular labour relations laws which the Thatcher government had initiated.

Some interest groups in Britain also engage in protest activities. The large-scale march through London and rally in Trafalgar Square is a familiar scene in British political history. The Campaign for Nuclear Disarmament (CND) organized regular marches in the 1950s, 1960s and 1980s. Somewhat less familiar, though by no means unknown, is illegal activity carried out in the name of civil disobedience. The Committee of One Hundred carried out illegal but non-violent activities, such as blocking roads, because it felt that the legal protests of the CND would be ineffective. Protest marches to denounce the policies of the United States in South East Asia in the late 1960s and very early 1970s were accompanied by the not entirely non-violent activities of splinter groups which tried to storm the American Embassy in Grosvenor Square.

Interest Groups and the European Community

As the use of European courts suggests, British interest groups are paying more attention in general to European institutions. Several important policies affecting Britain are now made within the framework of the institutions of the European Community in Brussels rather than in London; agricultural, trade and health and safety policies are obvious examples. It follows that British interest groups must work with their counterparts in other European countries to influence decisionmaking in the European Community. The NFU was predictably (given the importance of the Community's Common Agricultural Policy) a leader in this regard, helping to establish COPA, a confederation of farmers' organizations from the member countries, as an effective group. The NFU today realizes that it may obtain a friendlier hearing from the minister of agriculture of a country which has a significant farm vote than from the British minister of agriculture, who may be more constrained by consumers' or taxpayers' interests. The CBI has also established close working relations at the Community level with other employers' groups. Even the trade unions have started to overcome their distaste for working with foreigners and have started to establish more of a presence within the Community. Although the European Community's structure includes an Economic and Social Committee which is expressly designed to give interests a chance to comment on Community policies (most of its members being drawn from the ranks of interest group leaders), interest groups know that the real decisions are made in the Council of Ministers. Interest groups therefore concentrate on lobbying the European civil servants who draw up proposals for the Council and the ministers on the Council itself.

The importance of European institutions to British interest groups can only increase. The commitment to a truly common market within the EC in 1992 has brought home to many interests – especially companies – the potential impact of the Community's policies on their commercial activities. Trends in international trade policy also point to a dominant role for Community rather than national negotiators. Playing an effective role in Europe will be a challenge for interest groups, not least because, as the NFU has already discovered, being represented in Brussels is expensive.

More interest groups, like the NFU, will have to develop alliances with their equivalents in other Community countries. Yet the challenge cannot be avoided because the Community will make an increasing impact on interest groups. Some interests may also find that defeat in London can be offset by victories in Brussels, as the more alert British union leaders argued in the late 1980s.

Choosing a Strategy: Insider and Outsider Groups

It is generally held that not all strategies followed by interest groups in Britain are open to them simultaneously. In particular, it is thought by most observers that there is a conflict between close consultation and influence with the civil service and ministers on the one hand and campaigning, demonstrating and being actively involved in party politics on the other hand. The differences between these strategies have been conveniently summarized by Grant,[14] who refers to them as 'insider' versus 'outsider' strategies. Insider strategies turn on behaving in such a way that access to ministers and civil servants will be accorded to the interest group; outsider strategies involve campaigning, protest or partisan activities which generally result in denial of such access. It would also be argued by most observers that 'insider' status is the better strategy for influence, given the dominance of the executive in British policymaking. Given the improbability of defeating the government in the House of Commons, it is worth giving up a lot in order to maximize the opportunities to persuade it in private.

Yet not all British interest groups attempt to obtain insider status. Some British interest groups are by nature campaigning organizations that concentrate on attempting to bring about not some modest adjustment of policy today but some much more dramatic policy change tomorrow. The Campaign for Nuclear Disarmament (CND) is the most obvious but far from only example of a group which has chosen outsider rather than insider status. In large part, such choices reflect a realistic assessment of

---

[14] Grant, 'Insider Groups, Outsider Groups'; Grant, 'The Role of Interest Groups in Britain', in R. Borthwick and J. Spence (eds), *British Politics in Perspective*, Leicester University Press, Leicester, 1984.

the improbability of achieving the group's objectives through dialogue with ministers or civil servants. However, as James Q. Wilson has noted, some organizations attract individuals looking for solidaristic or expressive satisfactions rather than the achievement of specific policy changes.[15] Such individuals are more likely to be satisfied by demonstrations than by assurances that their leaders are engaged in fruitful dialogue with policymakers.

It is also true that the Labour Party is a powerful magnet for outsider groups. The CND is a good example of an organization which started out as non-partisan but ended up as an ally of the Labour Party. Women's organizations, which in the United States have maintained some non-partisan character, have likewise become closely associated with the Labour Party in Britain. Even the British National Council for Civil Liberties (NCCL) has been careful not to antagonize the Labour Party by supporting people who lost their jobs because they refused to join a union on conscientious grounds (a freedom more recently secured by the Thatcher government's labour laws). It is instructive to compare the British NCCL with its American counterpart, the ACLU, which has cheerfully antagonized politicians from both parties by supporting the rights of radicals of the left and the right (including Nazis and Oliver North).

Unions offer a fascinating example of a group torn between insider and outsider status. Most general secretaries of the Trades Union Congress (TUC) have valued insider status, believing that they could best serve their members by having access to policymakers. Indeed, it was the proud boast of one general secretary that he had brought the unions out of Trafalgar Square (where large demonstrations are often held) and into Whitehall (where government departments are located). It is interesting to speculate why British unions have been willing to abandon insider status. Perhaps part of the answer, as we noted above, is that British union leaders still think of themselves as part of a movement to transform society rather than as being pragmatists. It is also true that unions have provided a home for the far left in British politics (it is not uncommon to find that a minority of union leaders are Communists) and the far left has little interest in the reformist politics of negotiation and compromise of insider

[15] James Q. Wilson, *Political Organizations*, Basic Books, New York, 1974.

interest group politics. Unions have also perhaps over-estimated their ability to cow governments into surrender through a policy of non-co-operation or non-compliance with government policy. Whenever unions have suffered a major political reversal (such as the introduction of legislation limiting their powers) the left in the unions has been able to demand a greater emphasis on outsider political strategies, such as non-compliance with legislation or non-co-operation with government in a wide range of areas in which unions are closely consulted and greater emphasis on participation in the Labour Party. The history of the unions' opposition to the Heath government's reforms of industrial relations law is a case in point.[16] It should also be noted, however, that Mrs Thatcher was not at all distressed by having fewer contacts with union leaders.

The Nature of the British Interest Group System

So far we have been describing the tactics and strategies of interest groups. How might we characterize the interest group system in general? As we noted at the outset, the British interest group system at first glance looks much more unified and less competitive than the American system. The Confederation of British Industry is more or less secure as the spokesperson for employers (even though the more *laissez faire* Institute of Directors gained somewhat in status during the Thatcher government). The Trades Union Congress is completely unchallenged as spokesperson for labour, while the National Farmers' Union has only small (the Country Landowners' Association) or regional (the Farmers' Union of Wales) rivals. It is much easier in Britain than in the United States to identify one interest group which is *the* spokesperson for a sector of society.

Closer examination reveals more complications, however. In the first place, neither the CBI nor the TUC have any ability to make commitments on behalf of their members unless given express authority to do so. Both organizations are closer to being loose confederations than centralized interest groups which can force members to comply with agreements the parent body has

---

[16] Michael Moran, *The Politics of Industrial Relations*, Macmillan, London, 1977.

made. This characteristic of the TUC and CBI has had major implications for the possibility of running incomes policies or neocorporatist economic planning in Britain. No matter how sincerely leaders of the TUC might promise to abide by a limit on the pay increases which unions would seek, they could not force a determined minority of unions to comply. No matter how agreeable the leaders of the CBI might be in discussions for indicative economic planning, they could not guarantee that the firms within the CBI would invest on the scale necessary to meet the plan they had helped to make. In short, leaders have very little authority over members in both the CBI and TUC.

The layer of economic interest groups below the level of the peak associations is even more fragmented. The British trade unions have long been notorious for their number and overlapping jurisdictions (which when unions were stronger often led to severe labour disputes about which member of which union did what job). Most unions are themselves underfunded, ill-equipped to carry out serious analysis of even such issues as health and safety at work which affect members directly, yet are also jealous of any authority claimed by the TUC. Thus the TUC struggles to provide policy analysis with inadequate resources which the individual unions are reluctant to increase while they themselves rarely contribute much analysis or information to political debate.

Less well known but as important as the disarray among unions is the disarray among trade associations representing employers in a single industry. As the Devlin Commission reported to the CBI, trade associations are often in competition with another organization claiming to represent the same industry, are underfunded and ill-equipped to participate in policymaking. Of course, this generalization does not fit all industries. Some trade associations are impressive, gathering useful information, analysing clearly the problems of the industry and speaking authoritatively on behalf of members. Such trade associations are, however, probably a minority.[17] During the Thatcher years, the CBI has been threatened by the antagonism of the prime minister and her closest supporters, who believe it is too corporatist an organization and insufficiently committed to entrepreneurship,

[17] Grant, 'Insider Groups, Outsider Groups'.

and by a tendency for large corporations to develop their own capacities for political action.

Even more difficult for the CBI has been the special position of financial institutions in Britain. The separation between financial institutions and manufacturing is probably greater in Britain than in any other industrialized country. Moreover, financial institutions have long been used to gaining privileged access to policymakers through the Bank of England, which has traditionally interpreted its role as representing government and the City of London to each other. Thus the governor of the Bank of England has frequently pressed the views or interests of financial institutions on government. These views and interests have been given added force by the economic strength of the City. Not only is the City one of the most successful of British export industries; it also has the ability to direct money rapidly overseas thus reducing the value of the British pound if it distrusts government economic policies. Financial institutions have traditionally played little part in the CBI, seeing it as good enough for manufacturers or retailers, no doubt, but much inferior to the City's own channels of influence. Having the governor of the Bank of England speak on one's behalf to the chancellor of the exchequer and the Treasury is better than having a trade association. Yet things may be changing. Moran argues that financial institutions are eager to develop better interest group representation themselves,[18] believing that the old pattern of indirect representation through the Bank of England no longer suffices. In large part, this change is due to changes in the role of the Bank of England, which, since the adoption of monetarist policies in the late 1970s, has been a much more direct instrument of government policy than in the past. Inevitably, therefore, the governor of the Bank of England has been under closer government control, and has been less free to represent financial institutions to the government. Moreover, financial institutions themselves have changed considerably in recent years. The 'Big Bang' of de-regulation changed the City considerably, and the advent of Japanese, American and European financial institutions in the City has inevitably made its relationship with the British govern-

---

[18] Michael Moran, 'Finance capital and pressure group politics', *BJPolS*, 11, (1981), pp. 381–404.

ment less cosy. Yet there are no signs of financial institutions identifying more with the CBI. Their independence has had a strongly depressing effect on the standing of the CBI because the CBI is known not to represent such an important sector in the British economy.[19]

It was on these shaky foundations that British governments in the 1960s and 1970s attempted to build something like a neocorporatist mode of economic policymaking. By the early 1960s, it was fashionable to explain Britain's poor economic performance in terms of its failure to engage in indicative economic planning on the French model. Steps towards indicative economic planning were taken by the Macmillan government, which created the National Economic Development Council (NEDC) in 1963 to promote partnership between employers, unions and government in increasing the rate of economic growth. The 1964–70 Labour government adopted the format of a National Plan (obviously on the French model) and in order to smooth its formulation promoted the establishment of the CBI as the single authoritative voice of employers. Although the Plan was soon abandoned, the Labour government maintained close ties with the TUC, CBI, individual unions and trade associations. After initially disdaining neocorporatist links to economic interest groups, the Heath government (1970–4) rebuilt such links inspite of its conflicts with unions over labour legislation and the future of the coal industry. The 1974–9 Labour governments were strongly committed to partnership with the major economic interest groups, particularly the unions, in what they called a Social Contract. Even the CBI, however, was able to obtain major concessions from the Labour government, such as the quiet dumping of proposals for worker participation in the running of companies.

The Thatcher government is therefore distinctive in its repudiation of neocorporatist links with major economic interest groups. Thatcher has been explicit in expressing her dislike of neocorporatist arrangements, which conflict sharply with her

[19] On the tendency for the interests of finance capital to triumph over the interests of manufacturing in Britain, see Frank Longstreth, 'The city, industry and the state', in Colin Crouch (ed.), *State and Economy in Contemporary Capitalism*, Croom Helm, London, 1979.

philosophy of government as well as her belief in the superiority of market forces over any form of planning. Thatcher's approach has been based on a belief that British industry needs more entrepreneurship, not more tri-partite committees. Thus a government white paper published in 1988 made an amusing foray into political economy by attacking corporatism, which had hurt 'the ability of the economy to change and adapt', 'limited competition and the birth of new firms' whilst 'encouraging protectionism and restrictions designed to help existing firms'.[20] The government's relations with all the economic interest groups have been cool. The views of unions on economic policy as well as industrial relations legislation have been ignored. As we have seen above, relations between Thatcher and the CBI in the early 1980s were probably the worst between any prime minister and that body. The prime minister and her Cabinet systematically downgraded the importance of the NEDC; Thatcher was the first prime minister since its formation to refuse to attend its meetings regularly. In 1987, the government announced that the NEDC would itself meet less often and its staff would be reduced. This announcement was widely seen as the end of an era. Although it is harder to monitor, it seems as though relations between individual departments and major interest groups (e.g., the National Farmers' Union and the Ministry of Agriculture) are also less close than in the past. The restructuring of the Department of Trade and Industry in 1988 had as one of its explicit objectives the weakening of ties between sections of the Department and trade associations, ties which were seen as too corporatist.[21]

Yet the Thatcher government's repudiation of neocorporatism should be seen as the triumph of a tendency in British government rather than as a revolutionary break with the recent past. Although a neocorporatist spirit characterized dealings between British government and economic interests in the 1960s and 1970s, neither Labour nor Conservative politicians wholeheartedly embraced neocorporatist modes of thinking. Both the 1964–70 Labour and 1970–4 Conservative governments tried unsuccess-

[20] Department of Trade and Industry, *DTI – The Department for Enterprise*, Cmnd 278, HMSO, London, 1988. It is also amusing to note that this was the worst printed British government document I have ever seen.

[21] *DTI – The Department for Enterprise*.

fully to impose reforms in industrial relations legislation on unions. Edward Heath was frequently tempted by a style of government which would be based on firm authoritative leadership rather than compromise with interest groups. Even Harold Wilson talked occasionally of the 'smack of firm government'; he also abandoned the National Plan negotiated with employers and unions in 1965 and attempted, albeit unsuccessfully, to impose reform on the unions. Thus the question which should be explored is not only why Thatcher broke with neocorporatism but why neocorporatist arrangements have been both so tempting for British governments and yet so shallowly rooted.

Explaining the British Interest Group System

Several factors facilitated the moves towards neocorporatism in Britain. In the first place, the political culture and existing governmental practices were conducive to steps in that direction. The legitimacy of functional representation in Britain, as Beer noted, has deep roots. Indeed, the acceptance of functional representation may be seen in arguments against the 1832 Reform Act or the demands for representation of the American colonists the eighteenth century based on the idea of 'virtual' representation. The belief in the value of the representation of interests rather than opinions might indeed be associated with English constitutional thought since the debates about the appropriate roles of Commons, Lords and King in the seventeenth century. Second, as we noted above, British government departments, staffed with generalists and possessing little technical expertise, have been drawn into partnership with interest groups out of necessity. Such basic features of British life as the motorway system are based on advice supplied long ago by interest groups, in this case the civil engineers. Both beliefs about the desirability of consulting interests closely and the practical necessity for a state apparatus lacking technical expertise to seek their advice drew government departments into close partnership with interest groups.

A further consideration which promoted neocorporatism in Britain was the apparent necessity of operating an incomes policy. Until the Thatcher government, it was widely assumed in Britain that no government could withstand unemployment running at

Table 3.4 Opinions on the representativeness of union leaders in Britain

'Trade union leaders are out of touch with the workers they represent.'

	1986	1985
Agree	61	62
Disagree	26	28
Don't know	13	10

Source: SSLT (Gallup), 1986

more than 5 per cent. In general, unemployment should be substantially less than that. In such tight labour market conditions, unions would be able to obtain inflationary wage settlements unless government sponsored (and even enforced) limits on wage increases could be imposed. Such limits could be neither sensibly devised nor imposed without considerable co-operation from employers and unions, co-operation which the TUC and CBI would ensure. Yet the CBI, and particularly the TUC, could not be expected to confine their interests to setting limits on wage increases. The TUC in particular, like its counterparts in Sweden, would demand a wide variety of policy concessions in return for its co-operation on wage limits. Thus, full employment without inflation required neocorporatist discussions in which a wide variety of social and economic policies would be negotiated by government with interest groups.

Several factors also militated against neocorporatism in Britain. First, although functional representation was more widely accepted in the British than the American political culture, it was still not entirely legitimate. Beliefs in the sovereignty of the elected parliament conflicted with the neocorporatist practice of making concessions to economic interest groups. When in the 1970s Winkler announced in *The Times* that Britain had a corporatist form of government, his discovery was seen as cause for alarm. Neocorporatism was less compatible with British than with Swedish notions of democracy. No doubt such doubts about the desirability of neocorporatism are fuelled by the widespread doubts about the representativeness of the leaderships of economic groups in general, and unions in particular, as table 3.4 suggests.

Second, as might have been predicted from our discussions above of the strength of interest groups, British interest groups have not been able to deliver the compliance with policies which they endorse and which governments needed. The clearest example of this general problem is provided by unions. The TUC might have been convinced of the need for a given limit on wage increases in the days of incomes policies, but could not guarantee the compliance of member unions. Pressed for an explanation of their failure to co-operate, leaders of the individual unions often argued that they in turn could not guarantee the good behaviour of lower level officials of the unions such as shop stewards. Power was thus too decentralized in British unions to make their effective participation in incomes policy possible. The Labour government of 1974–9 ultimately foundered on the inability of unions to maintain an incomes policy that had been very successful in reducing inflation. The TUC explained that it could no longer hold in check individual unions; individual unions argued they could no longer keep in check their members and locally elected officials. Similarly, experience in the 1960s and 1970s showed that no amount of discussion with the CBI or trade associations would guarantee real economic action, such as increased investment, by employers. Thus the apparently impressive peak organizations representing economic interests in Britain proved to be broken reeds when government tried to lean on them. As the limitations of interest groups as an aid to government became more evident, so the appeal of working closely with them diminished. Indeed, the growth in the size and importance of technical branches of the civil service, such as the Economics Service, reduced the dependence of government departments on advice from interest groups compared with the situation described by political scientists in the early 1960s. British government today is not omniscient but is less technically ignorant than it used to be.

Whether or not these trends would have produced a major reduction in the importance of interest groups even if Mrs Thatcher had not become prime minister can be debated. A Callaghan government, re-elected in 1978 or after allowing a pre-election surge of incomes in 1979, may have sought to re-establish ties with the CBI and TUC. King has suggested that a Conservative prime minister other than Thatcher might have continued the neocorporatist arrangements of the recent past.[22] Yet it is hard to believe that any government would have placed as much faith in the value of neocorporatist arrangements as had been common in the 1960s and 1970s. Whatever the normative appeal or repulsion of neocorporatist arrangements, the British interest group structure had not proved strong enough to support them.

Non-economic Interest Groups

The discussion of British interest groups so far has centred on economic groups – unions, employers' organizations and representatives of special industries such as the National Farmers' Union. This concentration is legitimate because the British interest group system, especially the system of 'insider' groups enjoying privileged access to decisionmakers, has been dominated by economic groups.

Yet it is important to remember that although the British do not make as much fuss about their importance as do Americans, Britain also supports a lively collection of non-economic interest groups. The RSPB, (the Royal Society for the Protection of Birds) with half a million members recruits more individuals than does any British political party. Indeed, the strength of the voluntaristic streak in British political culture can be illustrated by the fact that several functions which might well be state functions are in fact dominated by voluntary organizations. The Royal Society for the Prevention of Cruelty to Animals (RSPCA) is the leading agency for animal welfare, the National Society for the Prevention of Cruelty to Children (NSPCC) is a leading agency in child welfare, and, most remarkably of all, the major surface sea rescue agency is the Royal National Lifeboat Institution (RNLI), which, as its advertisements state, is supported entirely by voluntary contributions.

Non-economic interest groups, like economic interest groups, can be divided into insider and outsider organizations. The insider group again has close even intimate working relations with

---

[22] Anthony King, 'What Thatcher has done to Beer', Paper presented to the Annual Convention of the American Political Science Association, Washington Hilton, Washington DC, 1986.

the relevant government department. Contacts with backbench members of parliament or public demonstrations are rare. Respectability is rewarded with the opportunity to influence ministers and civil servants when government policy is still in the more pliable initial stages. It is often possible to find in the same area as an 'insider' non-economic group an outsider group, eschewing the embrace of government and waging more public, highly political tactics and quite frequently resorting to direct action. Thus the RSPCA is regarded as hopelessly staid and corrupt by members of the League Against Cruel Sports and the members of direct action groups who release animals destined for laboratory tests. It is equally possible to find examples of areas monopolized by either an insider or outsider group. Thus there is no 'outsider' group on marine safety to compete with the RNLI and no 'insider' group which competes with CND in urging unilateral nuclear disarmament on the Ministry of Defence through more official channels.

Perhaps the most important of the non-economic insider groups are those such the National Trust, the RSPCA, NSPCC, or the RNLI which carry out non-political functions and for whom influencing policy is their secondary objective. Government must value such insider groups not only for their undoubted expertise but because they fulfil responsibilities which would otherwise fall on government; presumably were the RNLI not to exist, the Coast Guard would have to take on its responsibilities, as does the Coast Guard in the United States, which operates the American maritime rescue service. Non-economic groups which primarily seek to influence policy in reality have little to offer government. The Foreign Office is unlikely to find CND a useful source of information, no matter how respectably CND might try to behave. Finding themselves relatively unattractive to the bureaucracy, non-economic groups focusing on policy must take up the less promising tactics of protest marches, petitions, direct action, or lobbies of parliament and government in which they will often receive merely a *pro forma* hearing. There have indeed been non-economic interest groups which have seen their causes triumph; the campaigns to end the death penalty and relax the abortion laws are obvious examples. Anti-abortion rights groups and groups concerned to prevent shops opening on Sundays have recently made headway in parliament, perhaps in part because

British legislators are not used to dealing with vociferous minorities. Yet these movements have succeeded more because of sympathy for their causes among elite opinion in Britain than because of the strength of their support in the country. Indeed, the movement to tighten the abortion laws has mobilized many supporters without succeeding in changing the law.

It is not surprising, therefore, that political parties attract such policy-centred groups. Commitments made to gays, civil libertarians and CND in a Labour (or Liberal) Party manifesto may or may not be honoured in practice. The probability of success through influencing a political party which subsequently wins a General Election is greater, however, than the prospect of waging an independent campaign successfully. Yet success often remains a distant prospect, and as the history of CND has shown, it is extremely difficult for an interest group to maintain any general credibility once it has become closely associated with a single party. The TUC may be important enough to most governments to maintain, albeit with difficulty, both insider status and association with the Labour Party; CND is not.

The Future of the British Interest Group System

The image of the strength of British interest groups in the minds of most observers changed quite remarkably between the late 1970s and the late 1980s. The image in the late 1970s is set out most fully in Beer's later work, *Britain Against Itself*.[23] British government and society are torn by a war of all against all for higher subsidies, wages and any other advantage government can bestow. Even though the participants in the struggle can often recognize its irrationality, they are powerless to end it because the multiplicity of interest groups creates a prisoners' dilemma; a union considering forgoing an inflationary wage increase, for example, must bear in mind the fact that it can have no guarantee that the numerous competing groups will follow its example and show equal restraint. For its part, the state is seen as a helpless pitiful giant, 'overloaded' with demands from rapacious interest groups which it is powerless to either deny or, as it runs short

[23] Samuel Beer, *Britain Against Itself*, W. W. Norton, New York, 1982.

of resources, to meet. Recourse to the monetary printing press and acceptance of consequent inflation provide an escape from the overwhelming political and non-political pressures (e.g., strikes) which hem in the politicians.

Anyone who lived in Britain in the 1970s can recognize some validity at least in that picture of a British state overwhelmed by interest group power. No one who lived in Britain in the mid-1980s would find the account accurate. Beer's book has been described as one of the best books to become outdated almost overnight.[24] For the Thatcher government, as we have noted, has scarcely been polite, let alone paid deference, to interest groups. The CBI as well as the TUC have been banished from the chummy Downing Street chats with the prime minister which were so common under previous leaders. The machinery of consultation, such as the NEDC, has been allowed to decay. Above all, interest groups such as the National Union of Mineworkers, which challenged the authority of the state, have been defeated. The apparent balance of power between the state and interest groups has been reversed.

Much of this change is no doubt due to Mrs Thatcher. A less resolute leader might have backed away from confrontation with the miners rather than defeating them; as we noted above, some alternative Conservative prime ministers (Whitelaw, Pym, Prior) would have clung more tenaciously to more corporatist forms of interest group/government relations. Many of the same alternative Conservative prime ministers would have been attracted to an incomes policy in the hope of avoiding massive unemployment which Thatcher was prepared to accept. Such an incomes policy would have required a return to more neocorporatist modes of governance. Yet it would be unconvincing to attribute every change to one person, no matter how extraordinary a politician she might be. Deeper factors have been influencing the situation.

In the first place, as we noted, the events of the 1960s and 1970s seemed to show that interest groups were less valuable than they seemed. Neither the CBI nor TUC could in reality do much to secure the government's policy objectives. It followed that there was less reason to pay them a price for co-operation.

In the second place, the external constraints on the ability of

---

[24] King, 'What Thatcher has done to Beer'.

British governments to bargain with interest groups became clearer. It has rightly been remarked that many of the changes with which the Thatcher government is associated were started, though on a smaller scale, by the Callaghan government. This applies not only to monetarist economics but to government attempts to withstand public sector strikes. The most plausible explanation of the change is that British governments, forced into dependence on the International Monetary Fund for financial assistance in 1976, were forced to pay greater attention to the external economic constraints under which they operated and therefore to attach less significance to the domestic political forces operating upon them.

In the third place, the departure from full employment was extraordinarily liberating for British governments. The immediate effect of giving up the commitment to full employment was to make unnecessary incomes policies, which had been intended in the past to control inflation during periods of full employment. The refusal to have an incomes policy also freed the government from the need to co-operate with the CBI and TUC in forging and implementing such a policy, something which had been thought essential for implementing an incomes policy. Thus the whole apparatus of tri-partite negotiation could be downgraded in importance. Similarly, the Thatcher government's emphasis on market forces freed it from any need to work closely with trade associations or individual firms in organizing industrial restructuring, as had occurred in the 1960s and 1970s. A government which felt itself less responsible for the management of individual industries than had its predecessors had less need for co-operation or consultation with individual interests. Finally, the large increase in unemployment under Thatcher in and of itself reduced the power of trade unions, thereby diminishing their capacity to disrupt society on the scale witnessed in 1978–9.

It is easy to imagine, therefore, circumstances which encourage a return to a situation in which interest groups are more powerful again. Were Britain to regain full employment, the power of unions would be increased, even though the legal constraints on their power have been increased considerably since 1979. The arrival in power of a Labour government would encourage a tendency for employers to unite in face of the perceived dangers of Labour policies, whether or not those policies were implemented. For its part, a Labour government would welcome co-operation with an employers' organization in the hope that such co-operation would reduce the considerable risk of massive flights of capital from Britain. Operating the economy at full employment without inflation would be extremely difficult (wage increases remained high in Britain even when unemployment was considerable) without an incomes policy. Governments might again be attracted to neocorporatist bargaining with employers and unions in which all parties might hope to make gains – a return to full employment for unions, containing inflation for the government, and controlling costs or abating radical Labour policies for the employers.

British economic interest groups, for all their setbacks in the 1980s, still look strong and united by American standards. A single employers' organization, the CBI, clearly speaks for all sectors except finance. A single body, the Trades Union Congress, speaks for unions which still recruit 47 per cent of the workforce. The apparently strong peak associations will not go away. Governments of the future, particularly any government which attempts a more activist policy on incomes or industrial management, will be tempted to revive partnerships with economic interests which might make the task of economic management seem more manageable. Yet the lessons of the recent past suggest that neither employers' organizations nor unions would have the strength and internal cohesion to be capable of solving such difficulties. Indeed, economic interest groups which failed as building blocks of neocorporatism in the 1960s and 1970s have been weakened by what has happened since. The TUC has lost status as well as income as union membership has declined. Since the TUC expelled the (by Labour Party standards) right-wing electricians' trade union, it no longer even speaks for all major unions. A malaise has hung over the CBI after its confrontation with the Thatcher government in the early 1980s; the confrontation confirmed Mrs Thatcher's distaste for the administratively (as opposed to entrepreneurially) minded business executives in the CBI with their fondness for neocorporatist consultations. Major companies are turning increasingly to contract lobbyists to represent them rather than relying on trade associations or the CBI; a significant minority have also established an 'in-house' lobbying staff. The National Farmers' Union, once the exemplar of neocorporatist possibilities in Britain, has been undermined by a decline in membership, agricultural surpluses and the enormous cost of the Common Agricultural Policy. No agreement with the CBI in and of itself will ever increase investment. No agreement with the TUC on incomes policy will withstand for long inter-union rivalries over wage levels. Britain, if Thatcherism ends, may well return to oscillations between moves towards neocorporatism and disappointed departures from it after it has been perceived to fail.[25]

[25] For a description of the 'corporatist temptation' in British political history, see Middlemass, *Politics of Industrial Society*.

4

The Neocorporatist Systems

Neocorporatism, it will be remembered from chapter 1, is a system in which policy is made and implemented in a partnership between government and the major interests in a society (usually business and labour) represented by a limited number of interest groups licensed or recognized by the state which enjoy a monopoly on the effective representation of their interests. Neocorporatist systems of interest representation contrast with pluralist systems in which a multiplicity of groups, often competing with each other to represent the same interest and always competing with each other for influence, form temporary alliances with other interest groups or government agencies on an *ad hoc* basis; governments receive pressure from interest groups whose power or standing they can do little to influence.

Neocorporatism is a relative tendency, not an absolute one. In other words, although we can say that some countries are more neocorporatist than others, it would be wrong to say that some countries are completely neocorporatist and others are completely non-neocorporatist. Even those countries which are regarded as highly neocorporatist have seen a number of issues handled in what is clearly not a neocorporatist manner. Thus in Norway issues such as abortion, storing military equipment for the US Marines to use to defend Norway in the event of war, handling business banks and, above all, whether or not Norway should join the European Community have not been contained within the neocorporatist system of which the country is so often seen as an exemplar. Similarly, the issue of whether wage earner funds should acquire the stock of Swedish corporations over the long term or whether the corporations should remain in private hands could not be contained within the normal, neocorporatist framework.[1] Undoubtedly a considerable degree of segmentation exists so that the politics of different policy areas in neocorporatist countries can be quite distinct.[2] In contrast, it has been suggested that certain issues in countries which are not normally considered at all neocorporatist may be handled in a neocorporatist manner. Although most of the neocorporatist theorists, such as Schmitter, rank Britain very low on lists of the most neocorporatist nations, there is no doubt that public policy on a number of issues as diverse as occupational safety and health and agricultural production has been made in a highly neocorporatist manner.[3] To add to our difficulties, countries may vary over time in the degree to which they are neocorporatist, passing through periods in which their interest groups system is more or less neocorporatist. Thus, some see in the rise of issues in Sweden which cannot be kept within the neocorporatist framework a trend towards the breakdown of the entire neocorporatist system. In Britain in the late 1960s and 1970s, commentators read into the frequency and range of negotiations between government and unions a permanent trend towards neocorporatism which in fact came to an abrupt end with the election of the Conservatives in 1979.

Finally, although our discussion so far has been set in terms of the interest group system of *nations*, it is important to note that much recent research has focused on the manner in which *industrial sectors* are represented in different nations. This research opens up the interesting possibility that certain industrial sectors, for example, the dairy industry, are represented in a neocorporatist manner in a variety of countries with very different political systems. Neocorporatism may be found not at the national but at the 'meso' level at which individual industries interact with government. The focus is therefore not so much on umbrella organizations representing employers or unions but on trade

[1] Robert Kvavik, *Interest Groups in Norwegian Politics*, Universitetsforlaget, Oslo, 1976; Bernd Marin, 'Austria – the paradigm case of liberal corporatism?', in Wyn Grant (ed.), *The Political Economy of Corporatism*, Macmillan, Houndmills, 1985; Hugh Heclo and Henrik Madsen, *Policy and Politics in Sweden*, Temple University Press, Philadelphia, 1987. Heclo and Madsen in fact deny that corporatism is the best way to conceptualize Swedish politics.
[2] Johann Olsen, *Organized Democracy; Political Institutions in a Welfare State*, Universitetsforlaget, Oslo, 1983.
[3] See Graham K. Wilson, *The Politics of Safety and Health*, Oxford University Press, Oxford and New York, 1985.

associations representing an industry, unions within that industry and individual government departments. The focus on the meso level has the advantage of making visible neocorporatist patterns of policymaking which might be obscured in focusing on the national level particularly when a system is not in general neocorporatist.

Yet a focus on the 'meso' level also has important disadvantages. At the end of the day, someone has to summarize the findings about different industries in an account of the system in general. It is interesting to know that the dairy industry in a particular country is neocorporatist while the steel industry is not. Those who study comparative politics are still likely to ask whether the political system as a whole is, or is not, neocorporatist. Are industries governed in a neocorporatist manner more numerous, less numerous, more important or less important than those which are not? Moreover, a focus on the 'meso' level might legitimately be seen as trivializing the original concept of neocorporatism. Claims that entire political systems were neocorporatist had major significance in two respects. First, the claim that a system was neocorporatist had normative implications in that it suggested that electoral politics were less significant than had been assumed. Rokkan's famous comment that in Norway 'elections count, resources decide'[4] was a normatively significant statement that interest group politics matter more than electoral. Elections, Rokkan meant, had consequences, but the consequences of elections were not as important as the dealings between interest groups speaking for those with resources and the government. The interest group system was more important than the electoral system. Second, neocorporatism at the national level could be understood as settling class conflict through institutional means. It is interesting to note that both Austria and Sweden, exemplars of neocorporatism, had histories of considerable, and in the case of Austria violent, class conflict before neocorporatist modes of compromise were developed. It would seem, therefore, that contrary to the direction of much current neocorporatist research,

[4] Stein Rokkan, 'Norway, numerical democracy and corporate pluralism', in Robert Dahl (ed.), *Political Oppositions in Western Democracies*, Yale University Press, New Haven, 1966.

a focus on the degree to which *countries*, as opposed to *industries*, are neocorporatist is desirable.

As has already been noted, it is generally accepted that some countries are more neocorporatist than others. Attempts to scale countries according to their degree of neocorporatism have produced somewhat contradictory results.[5] However, it is commonly agreed that the list of the most neocorporatist countries includes Austria, the Scandinavian countries (amongst whom Denmark is probably less neocorporatist than Norway or Sweden), the Netherlands and probably Belgium. Katzenstein would somewhat controversially add Switzerland to the list.[6]

West Germany is a most interesting marginal case. In spite of a period in which the country was theoretically committed to policies such as the social market economy and anti-monopoly practices which seemed not at all neocorporatist, enduring tendencies towards concentration in the economy and its direction by administrative rather than market mechanisms have frequently produced what may legitimately be termed neocorporatist arrangements for administering certain sectors of the economy. Banks, rather than government, may take the leadership role, but major policy questions are still settled by representatives of the major economic interests and government. In West Germany as in Britain, the late 1960s and early 1970s witnessed a substantial upturn in the degree to which the economy could be characterized as neocorporatist with the institutionalization of consultation between government, employers and unions over the direction of the economy. Indeed, this growth of neocorporatism might well be understood as a return to the traditional German pattern, visible in both the Weimar Republic and Nazi regime, though temporarily obscured by the emphasis immediately after the Second World War on a market-orientated approach. Thus Professor Gerhard Fels, a member of a research institute associated with the Confederation of German Industry, has argued: 'Germany has always been the land of cartels, under the Nazis and in the

---

[5] For examples see Suzanne Berger (ed.), *Organizing Interests in Western Europe*, Cambridge University Press, Cambridge, 1981 and John Goldthorpe (ed.), *Order and Conflict in Contemporary Capitalism*, Oxford University Press, Oxford, 1982; Wyn Grant, *The Political Economy of Corporatism*, Macmillan, Houndmills, 1985.

[6] Peter Katzenstein, *Small States in World Markets*, Cornell University Press, Ithaca, 1985.

Weimar Republic. Now we have become again what we have always been – corporatists.'[7]

At least at first sight, the countries which have been named so far as the most neocorporatist might seem to comprise a most diverse collection. Certainly there are important differences in their histories and political traditions. Sweden and Norway emerged as modern democracies in a manner reminiscent of Britain. That is to say, a monarchy in which the king or queen had ruled in partnership with the more privileged sectors of society was gradually transformed into a modern, parliamentary democracy in which power is exercised by democratically elected governments. By and large these transitions, including the emergence of Norway as an independent state, were achieved peacefully. The history of modern Austria is very different. The First Austrian Republic (1919–38) was one of the most troubled of the European states. Violent conflicts between left and right defeated attempts to establish the legitimacy of the new state, all that was left after the disastrous dissolution of the Austro-Hungarian Empire following the First World War. Austria polarized into political parties which reach so deep into society that they have been called 'camps'. In 1933, the Chancellor, Dollfuss, the leader of the Catholic Party, suspended the Constitution and created a fascist state which in 1933 forcefully repressed the Social Democrats. The absorption of Austria into Germany by Hitler, the *Anschluss*, was welcomed by most Austrians, (though it led to persecution and death for both Austria's Jews and many Socialists). After the war, though occupied by the Great Powers until 1955, Austria was generally regarded as a victim of Nazism, and was allowed its freedom by the Powers under the 1919 Constitution but usually referred to as the Second Republic. The Netherlands, another constitutional monarchy, has maintained domestic tranquillity despite the potential for conflict rooted in the division of the country into Catholic and Protestant communities each with its own parties, interest groups and unions. The maintenance of peace and tolerance in spite of these divisions through 'consociational practices' has rightly attracted the attention of political scientists only too aware of the potential in such differences for conflict in other settings such as Northern Ireland.

[7] *Financial Times*, 5 November 1987.

The history of modern Germany is too familiar to need summariz-
ing, but again contrasts with the orderliness of Scandinavian or
Dutch history.

What are the conditions for the existence of a neocorporatist
interest group system? Several factors are obvious. First,
neocorporatist systems are nearly always found in societies in
which social class has constituted an important division. Social
democratic parties have won a major share of the vote in
Germany, Norway, Sweden and Austria. The Swedish Social
Democrats have governed Sweden since 1935 with only brief
interruptions, such as 1976–80. The Austrian Social Democrats
(Socialistiche Partei Österreichs) captures about half the vote, the
remainder going mainly to the Osterreichs Volks Partei while the
Liberal Party (Freiheitliche Partei Osterreichs) wins 5.5–8 per
cent of the vote. The German Socialist Party (Socialistiche Partei
Deutsch) has not won a majority of the vote since 1945 but has
been able to govern in coalition with the Free Democrats on two
occasions. Indeed, neocorporatist arrangements can be understood
in part as one way to cope with class divisions – by institutionalized
compromise. It has been said, somewhat ironically, that social
class divisions have two immense political advantages.[8] Class
differences are relatively few (generally the somewhat richer
against the somewhat poorer) whereas other differences (e.g.,
regional) can be legion; class differences can also be compromised
(e.g., through redistributive policies). The presence of numerous
divisions in society might make neocorporatist arrangements
impossible to attain as too many interests and interest groups
might claim the right to be involved. Certain non-economic issues
(e.g., of which nation should Northern Ireland be part) are of
their very nature unamenable to compromise. The neocorporatist
countries therefore gain from the dominance of their politics by
social class a reduction in the number of potential issues; moreover,
the dominant issue is amenable to compromise. However, it
must be admitted that religious divisions in the Netherlands and
language conflicts in Belgium have constituted important divisions
cutting across class conflicts which have been more and less
successfully resolved in the two countries respectively. None the

---

[8] Wolfgang Streeck, 'Neocorporatist industrial relations and the economic crisis in West
Germany', in Goldthorpe (ed.), *Order and Conflict.*

less, social class has played an important part in shaping the parties and interest group systems of even these two countries so that socialist parties are strong and unions recruit a high proportion of potential members. There may have been Catholic and Protestant, Walloon and Flemish socialist parties or unions, but their strength has still been significant.

A second prerequisite for the existence of neocorporatist systems is the existence of relatively few, relatively centralized interest groups representing the major economic interests. Whether or not neocorporatist systems can be created, or are available only to countries which already possess a suitable interest group system can be debated. One school of thought, represented by Lehmbruch,[9] suggests that suitable interest group structures emerge gradually and cannot be created by governments. Another school would contend that states have the capacity to mould interest group structures. A variety of techniques can be used by states to foster more unified interest group systems. Governments can refuse to consult with any but the most important interest group in a policy area and can encourage by a variety of means (including, in Austria, legal compulsion) people to join the interest group representing their interests. Of course, in practice both the efficacy and legitimacy of attempts by government to strengthen a particular interest group will be greater in societies whose interest group structures are already relatively concentrated and centralized. Although the efforts of the state might turn an interest group system on the verge of neocorporatism into a neocorporatist system, it is unlikely that, except under the most unusual circumstances, states could restructure interest group systems at will. Certainly crises such as war or severe economic crisis have often brought about only a temporary increase in the degree to which the system is neocorporatist in uncongenial settings such as the USA. Such critical moments may have been important in promoting neocorporatism, while their relative infrequency might also mean that neocorporatism is not for export.

A third condition for the establishment of neocorporatist arrangements might be the presence of a willingness to compromise among interest group leaders and government officials. Indeed, it

[9] Gerhard Lehmbruch, 'Concertation and the structure of corporatist networks', in Goldthorpe (ed.), *Order and Conflict*.

has been said in Austria that neocorporatism should be understood not as a set of institutional practices but as a habit of never making an important policy change without consulting and negotiating widely. Consultation, negotiation and compromise might require a formal meeting or it might only require a chat while sitting on the park bench; however much consultation or negotiation is required must take place. Negotiating and compromising are habits deeply ingrained in the Swedish policy-making process as the frequent use of Royal Commissions and the '*remiss*' procedure for consulting interest groups testify.[10] Before legislation is presented to parliament, the government attempts to reach a compromise with interested parties. Royal Commissions in Sweden are not, as in Britain, merely bodies set up to enquire into a situation. Composed of representatives of interested groups and government departments, Swedish Royal Commissions are bodies in which compromise solutions to problems can be negotiated. The *remiss* procedure involves the final draft of legislation being sent to interest groups for their comments which are presented to parliament along with the legislation. Even the legislative process itself is unusually geared to compromise for a parliamentary system, so that even the opposition parties can expect to have some impact on legislation. As noted above, such habits of compromise have not always been present in Austria and Sweden but may be seen as the residue of periods of conflict and crisis. In the case of Austria, the intense conflict which characterized the final years of the First Republic and which helped to bring about the *Anschluss* with Nazi Germany produced a determination in the post-war years to manage conflict amicably. The occupation of Austria by the victorious Allies (including the Soviet Union) until 1955 also produced a feeling that the independence of the country was precarious, a feeling not entirely ended by the conclusion of the occupation. Deep conflict as in the First Republic would endanger independence. Not only the political independence of Austria encouraged the spirit of compromise. As Katzenstein has noted,[11] small nations are extraordinarily dependent on foreign trade, and, though union leaders in Britain have not always accepted this,

---

[10] For a description of the process, see Heclo and Madsen, *Policy and Politics*.
[11] Katzenstein, *Small States*.

trade dependent countries can ill afford industrial conflict leading to disruption of exports. Compromise was an economic as well as a political necessity. Similarly, although Sweden experienced much industrial unrest during its period of rapid industrialization, the mature Swedish economy was also dependent for its extremely high living standards on the success of its exporting industries. Compromise between labour, capital and government was thus an economic necessity as well as a habit rooted in the Swedish political culture. Although it might be argued that the example of Britain in the period 1951–79 shows that not all countries dependent on trade realize the importance of avoiding industrial conflict, it can be argued both that Britain is the anomaly to be explained and that the trade dependence of small nations such as Austria is even greater than Britain's. Perhaps the willingness of German unions to compromise with employers has also been due to the dependence of the mighty German economy on exports.

A fourth characteristic of neocorporatist systems is widespread acceptance of functional representation, i.e., the belief that people's interests can be represented legitimately by economic organizations such as unions or employers' organizations as well as by elected politicians. Such acceptance of functional representation is not of course universal. Anyone who has tried to explain neocorporatist practices to articulate American students will know that in the United States, neocorporatist practices are frequently perceived as giving 'special interests' illicit opportunities to influence public policy. So called public interest groups, such as Common Cause, would no doubt bring legal action at once to halt any attempt to settle public policy in the private meetings between representatives of the major economic interests which neocorporatism entails. Similarly, claims in the 1970s that Britain was becoming neocorporatist prompted concerns that the power of parliament was thereby being eroded. Contrast this attitude with the practices of neocorporatism in Austria as described by Gerlich.

During the Second Republic the big economic interest groups have achieved a position of great power. Characteristically, the Chambers of Commerce, Labor and Agriculture (Handelskammer, Arbeiterkammer and Landwirtschaftskammer) have a kind of semi-official status in that every citizen economically active is by law considered a member. To these has been added the Federation of Trades Unions (Osterreicher Gewerkschaftsbund) which, though a voluntary body, has organized almost two thirds of all workers and holds a virtual monopoly of trade union representation. These four large organizations ... effectively practice consociational politics within the framework of the so-called Joint Commission (Paritatische Kommission), *which amounts to a second government for economic affairs. All wage and many price policies must, in fact, be approved by this body which does not have any constitutional or even legal basis.*[12]

Although, as we have seen, functional representation constitutes part of the British political tradition, another strong tendency in British political thought has been to call for reducing what seemed to many the excessive power of economic interest groups, such as unions in the 1970s; a neocorporatist response would have been to accept the power of unions but to incorporate them into policymaking. It is probably the case that functional representation is accepted most fully where its history is longest. Thus in both Austria and Germany, state encouragement, or even compulsion, of membership in economic organizations or Chambers (Kammern) can be traced back to the Middle Ages. The liberal upsurge of the 1848 revolutions in the Austro-Hungarian Empire had the effect of increasing the proportion of the population included in the Kammern system, not abolishing the system itself. Indeed, even today, nearly all the working population of Austria must by law belong to one of the Kammern.

A fifth prerequisite for the existence of neocorporatism is the existence of a relatively centralized state. Neocorporatist practices involve making authoritative bargains between economic interests and government. Bargains once made must be honoured. Such bargains are relatively difficult to make if, as in the United States, the state itself is fragmented into different competing, sometimes conflicting, institutions. As countries negotiating treaties with the United States have found, an agreement made in good faith by the executive branch might be disregarded by the Congress. Moreover, as noted above, fragmented states cannot build the standing of individual interest groups by restricting the access of

[12] Peter Gerlich, 'Government structure', in Kurt Steiner (ed.) *Modern Austria*, Society for the Promotion of Science and Scholarship, Palo Alto, California, 1981, pp. 217–18 (emphasis added).

their rivals to policymakers. An interest group denied access to one part of American government might still find a hearing elsewhere, thus reducing the incentive to build a more unified interest group system. Competing interest groups in turn, as Olson noted, will find it difficult to sacrifice short-term interests to long-term gains because there can be no guarantee that their rivals will behave in a similarly statesman-like manner. Only recurring or iterative bargaining between government and relatively few interests can solve the problem of the prisoners' dilemma in which fruitful, co-operative behaviour does not occur for fear that others will not behave in a co-operative manner also.

Such conditions for neocorporatism are met sufficiently in relatively few countries, although, as we have noted, neocorporatism is a relative tendency, not an absolute one. It is indeed difficult to believe that countries could deliberately bring about the conditions for full neocorporatism, though opportunities in specific policy areas may be greater.

The Performance of Neocorporatist Countries

Neocorporatist interest group systems would not have attracted so much academic interest if it had not seemed plausible to suggest that such systems were unusually effective. Some evidence on the comparative prosperity of different nations is presented in tables 4.1 and 4.2. The prosperity of Sweden, Norway and, more impressively because it started from a lower economic level, Austria, convinced many that neocorporatist countries were more economically successful as well as more domestically tranquil than less neocorporatist countries. Of course, it is very difficult to validate such claims because of the multiplicity of factors involved in explaining economic success or failure. Thus, Swedish economic growth in the 1950s and 1960s was partly a result of growing world trade; Austrian economic success was partly a spillover from the great strength of the West German economy. Advocates of neocorporatism, such as Schmitter, have argued however that such international factors are not the whole story. Less neocorporatist countries, such as Britain, failed to take advantage of the growth of world trade to the same degree as Sweden. Moreover, Schmitter argues, neocorporatist countries

Table 4.1 Gross national product per capita in constant (1983) dollars, 1975–84

Country	1975	1980	1984
USA	12,850	14,520	15,380
Austria	6,990	8,432	8,892
Belgium	7,285	8,286	8,372
France	8,111	9,364	9,510
Italy	5,306	6,326	6,330
Netherlands	8,605	9,462	9,338
Sweden	10,240	10,650	11,050
United Kingdom	7,262	7,799	8,270
West Germany	8,879	10,650	11,020
Norway	NA	12,689	12,930

Source: Statistical Abstract of the United States, US Department of Commerce, Bureau of the Census, Washington DC, 1988, from table 1387

Table 4.2 Tax revenue as a percentage of gross domestic product

Country	1975	1980	1983	1984	1985
USA	29	29.5	28.4	28.4	29.2
Austria	38.6	41.2	41.1	42.1	42.5
Belgium	41.1	43.6	45.5	46.5	46.9
Denmark	41.4	45.5	46.5	48.0	49.2
France	37.4	42.5	44.6	45.5	45.6
Italy	25.1	30.0	35.9	35.1	34.7
Japan	20.9	25.5	27.2	27.4	28.0
Netherlands	31.3	33.0	33.1	33.0	34.3
Norway	44.8	47.1	46.6	45.8	47.8
Sweden	43.9	49.4	50.6	50.3	50.5
Great Britain	35.4	38.0	37.3	37.5	37.8

Source: Statistical Abstract of the United States, Department of Commerce, Bureau of the Census, Washington DC, 1988, table 1397

were clearly more successful in responding to the hard times which the world economy brought to all countries in the 1970s. Neocorporatist countries, according to Schmitter, were able to avoid the peaks of inflation, the depths of unemployment, and the mountains of debt and even the civil unrest which plagued other democracies.[13] As Heclo and Madsen have noted, Sweden's economic problems seemed severe to Swedes in the 1970s; but they did not point out that many countries in that decade would have been glad to settle for Sweden's problems rather than their own.[14]

What was it about neocorporatist arrangements which produced such desirable results? The neocorporatist literature is somewhat silent on this point. However, an answer can be constructed. One arm of neocorporatist thinking would assert that contrary to popular liberal thinking, neocorporatist systems are better able to promote economic growth precisely because they are more organized. Technological developments can be more rapidly turned into successful commercial applications when highly organized, concentrated industries can co-operate with the financial sector and government to obtain the necessary resources. Organized economies succeed in adapting to economic change faster than market systems. Neocorporatist systems above all ensure that differences of interest do not become irreconcilable and so a source of conflicts so deep as to damage society. Neocorporatist arrangements secure social order through institutionalized compromise, whereas the Madisonian idea of restraining interests by setting against them countervailing interests is all too likely to spill over into damaging industrial conflicts or civil unrest. Finally, as we have emphasized above, the all-encompassing interest group is much better able to sacrifice the short-term interests of its members in order to secure their long-term interests than is the interest group which competes for members with others in the same field.

Neocorporatism was therefore a solution to the problem of governability which so many astute commentators discussed in

---

[13] Philippe Schmitter, 'Interest intermediation and regime governability in contemporary western Europe and North America', in Berger (ed.), *Organizing Interests in Western Europe*.

[14] Heclo and Madsen, *Policy and Politics*.

the 1970s. Writers in many countries in the 1970s sensed a shift in power away from governments towards interest groups. Governments were increasingly dependent on interest groups not merely in the formulation and implementation of public policy but in securing goals such as investment for economic growth, the avoidance of economic and social disruption caused by strikes and social stability. The crumbling of British economic life and social order during the repeated challenges of the miners' union to the Conservative government of 1970–4 seemed to demonstrate that the social order could be more easily disrupted today than in the past. How, King asked perceptively, could it be that a short miners' strike in 1973 and 1974 caused more dislocation than a lengthy miners' strike in 1926 when coal was clearly then a more important source of energy?[15] The answer was that in the 1970s, society could be more easily disrupted by many groups than in the 1920s; life had become more interdependent. To make matters worse, groups were making more and more demands on government, which was in consequence less and less able to meet them. The triumph of neocorporatism was to achieve social peace by reducing the number and irresponsibility of demands on government by inviting relatively few, relatively responsible interest groups capable of thinking beyond today to share in governing society.

Still the Century of Corporatism?

Schmitter, whose work is so central to the study of neocorporatism, in 1974 published an article with the same title as this subsection.[16] Schmitter concluded that it was. Throughout the 1970s, few could doubt that neocorporatism did seem to work. It was not surprising that certain developments in the 1970s in countries not normally thought of as neocorporatist seemed to indicate that they were consciously moving in that direction. President Nixon's wage–price freeze in the USA and the 'social contract' established in Britain by the 1974–9 Labour government are obvious

[15] Anthony King (ed.), *Why is Britain Becoming Harder to Govern?*, BBC Publications, London, 1976.
[16] Philippe Schmitter, 'Still the century of corporatism?', *Review of Politics*, 36, (1974), pp. 85–131.

examples. Neither, of course, worked for long or even particularly well. But their failure could be interpreted not as calling into question the value of neocorporatism but as illustrating the warnings of writers such as Schmitter and Lehmbruch that neocorporatist systems could not easily be created in other countries.

In the 1980s, neocorporatist systems displayed disadvantages as well as advantages as Schmitter himself noted. Three main lines of weakness have been apparent.

First, the organized nature of neocorporatist economies has been associated not with stability but with rigidity. Fast changing economic circumstances have been alleged to require greater mobility of capital and labour than rigidified neocorporatist systems provide. Neocorporatist economies such as Sweden saw their economic growth rates decline, something which economic commentators thought not coincidental. Indeed, in the 'post Fordist' phase of capitalism (i.e., when Benetton, which produces and sells clothes in small establishments, prospers while firms dependent on large-scale production languish), the concentrated economies of the neocorporatist states might well be at a disadvantage. At least between the early and late 1980s, it seemed that it was the American economy, the least neocorporatist of all systems, which seemed to show the greatest dynamism, creating millions of new jobs while western Europe added no net increase in jobs. The apparent recovery in the British economy in the mid-1980s under a Conservative government which had vigorously and explicitly renounced neocorporatist tendencies in theory and in practice, by measures such as the reduction of contacts with the TUC, CBI and the downgrading of the National Economic Development Council, again suggested that neocorporatism and economic growth were in conflict.

The second problem confronting neocorporatist systems is class decomposition. As the neocorporatist states have become richer, so it may be that the willingness of their workers to think of their interests as workers rather than as car workers, bank employees etc. has diminished. In this respect, neocorporatist systems may be, as Streeck has suggested, victims of their own economic success.[17] For one of the foundations of neocorporatism

[17] Streeck, 'Neocorporatist industrial relations'.

has been the ability of labour leaders to secure the restraint of those of their members who might be able to press for even higher wages in order to allow benefits to flow to less well-off workers. As class solidarity has weakened, so the willingness of stronger workers to make this sort of sacrifice has diminished. Thus, national wage bargaining, which formed the bedrock of Swedish neocorporatism, has broken down in recent years as workers in more successful industries have no longer been willing to forgo wage increases in order to help workers in weaker industries.

The third problem confronting the neocorporatist systems has been the rising costs of their welfare systems. The relationship between the scale of the welfare state in countries such as Sweden and the high degree of neocorporatism is not entirely coincidental. For one of the standard forms of neocorporatist bargaining has been for unions and employers to agree on wage restraint while the government rewards the unions with an increase in the 'social wage' of welfare benefits. Such bargains in the short term have helped to ensure industrial peace and contain wage increases in export industries. In the longer term, such bargaining faces two constraints. The first is that, in so far as the welfare state is financed by taxes on employers, the total labour costs of employers may increase to levels which make their products uncompetitive in the world economy. The second constraint is that, in so far as the welfare state is financed by taxes on individuals, the dangers of tax revolt arise. Even the citizens of Scandinavian countries have shown some restiveness about the extremely high levels of taxation which prevail in their countries. The Swedes had a non Social Democratic government from 1976 to 1980 while Denmark has seen even greater attrition in the strength of the left.[18] It is unlikely that there is much scope left for bargains which drive up the cost of the welfare state to taxpayers. Similarly, the resurgence of corporatism in Germany has been accompanied by mounting subsidies to powerful industrial sectors that are resented increasingly by other sectors which bear the burden of these subsidies. Subsidies to industries rose from just under DM 60 billion in the early 1970s to over DM 120 in the late 1980s while such features of poor economic performance as low growth rates

---

[18] Eric Einhom and John Logue, *Welfare States in Hard Times, Problems, Policy and Politics in Denmark and Norway*, Kent Popular Press, Kent, Ohio, 1982.

and high unemployment have become familiar.[19]

It is entirely possible that the advantages of neocorporatism were exaggerated because our image of the workings of neocorporatist societies was formed during the decades of constant economic growth from the Second World War until the 1970s. Awareness of the difficulties of operating neocorporatist systems in the much more difficult international economic climate since the mid-1970s may be a most useful corrective. Yet it would be a mistake if we exaggerated the difficulties faced by neocorporatist systems to the point where we assumed that the disappearance of neocorporatism is inevitable. To say that neocorporatism may be working less smoothly than hitherto is not to say that the system itself will vanish, nor that it may yet continue to perform better than might alternative systems.

Corporatism Without Labour?[20]

Is it legitimate to regard France and Japan as operating variants of neocorporatism? The argument in favour is clear. For most of the period since the Second World War, both countries have promoted economic growth through a close partnership between government and economic interests. The argument against using the neocorporatist label is equally clear. For in both countries trades unions, instead of being incorporated into the policymaking process, have generally been too weak for it to be necessary to compromise with them. Unions in France not only represent a small proportion of the workforce (less than 20 per cent) but are divided between Catholic, Socialist and Communist organizations. The same differences within the left which gave rise to separate Socialist and Communist Parties, and which divided the anti-clerical left from the practising Catholics resulted in separate union organizations – the Confédération Générale du Travail (the Communist CGT), the Confédération Française Démocratique du Travail (the Socialist CFDT) and the formerly Catholic, now independent, Force Ouvriers (FO). In Japan, after an upsurge of

[19] *Financial Times*, 4 November 1987.
[20] This is the title of T. J. Pempel's article on Japan in Gerhard Lehmbruch and Philippe Schmitter (eds), *Patterns of Corporatist Policymaking*, Sage Publications, London and Beverly Hills, 1982.

militant unionism was crushed shortly after the Second World War, that minority of workers which is unionized belongs predominantly to company unions, representing workers only within a single enterprise to which workers are often fiercely loyal. There have been moments, however, when unions in both countries have temporarily assumed greater importance. The economic pressures on western democracies in the 1970s resulted in political pressures on ruling groups, even in Japan and France. Both Japanese and French governments showed increased willingness to deal with at least some unions; in France the election of a Socialist president and parliamentary majority in the early 1980s gave unions a further though temporary boost in importance. These episodes should not cause us to revise our low estimate of the power of unions in these systems in general.

In fact, both Japan and France have several different interest group systems. As T. J. Pempel notes, 'the picture of Japan's political society as composed of big business, agricultural and labor groups is over-simplified. At various times, groups such as veterans, former landlords, senior citizens, students, environmentalists, doctors, war widows, teachers and numerous others have influenced political decisions'.[21] Pempel also notes that in the early 1970s there were 3,000 citizens' groups devoted to environmental issues while new groups were emerging to address problems such as consumer prices, the quality of consumer goods, education reform, increasing the role of local government and promoting rights for women. Chalmers Johnson notes that 'interest groups exist in Japan in great numbers'[22] and that one of the roles of the relatively weak parliament (Diet) has been to force the state to compromise with interests such as agriculture which could not be ignored.

Rice farmers are a celebrated example of an interest group which has achieved considerable benefits from government in return for votes for the ruling Liberal Democratic Party (LDP); these votes are particularly valuable because of the over-represen-

[21] T. J. Pempel, *Policy and Politics in Japan, Creative Conservatism*, Temple University Press, Philadelphia, 1982, p. 32.

[22] Chalmers Johnson, *MITI and the Japanese Miracle, the Growth of Industrial Policy, 1925–75*, Stanford University Press, Stanford, 1982, p. 49.

tation of rural interests in Japan.[23] Other vociferous interests such as the Japanese repatriated after the Second World War from land occupied by Japan were only partially successful, however.[24] Indeed, many writers now think that westerners have exaggerated the power of the Japanese state, which, Samuels argues, has succeeded by working with certain interest groups and market forces rather than attempting to impose its will on society.[25] The Japanese state negotiates more than it leads. Similarly in France, as is well known to followers of disputes within the European Community, farmers during the Fourth Republic were successful in extracting subsidies from politicians through the standard techniques of pluralist persuasion mixed with a little rioting; as we shall see, the relationship between farmers and the state changed significantly thereafter away from this pattern.

Yet no one thinks that either the French or Japanese political systems are pluralist in any sense that an American would recognize. In both countries interest groups not legitimated by the state are suspect. French political discourse has usually contrasted interest groups with supposedly selfish concerns with the public interest which is, or ought to be, promoted by the state. Similarly, as Chalmers Johnson notes, in Japan interest groups operate within a political culture which provides 'no theory of pluralism that legitimates their political activities'.[26] Moreover, certain interests – primarily business – are marked out as having exceptional status, opportunities to influence policymakers and power. These interests are primarily the representatives of big business.

In Japan, relations between the industrial leaders in both individual companies and the Federation of Economic Organizations, or *Keidanren*, which represents the collective interests of employers are eased by the practice of *amakudari*, recruitment practices and campaign finance.

---

[23] Michael Donnelly, 'Setting the price of rice: a study in political decisionmaking', in T. J. Pempel (ed.), *Policymaking in Contemporary Japan*, Cornell University Press, Ithaca, 1977.

[24] John Campbell, 'Compensation for expatriates: a case study of interest group politics and party government negotiation', in Pempel (ed.), *Policymaking in Contemporary Japan*.

[25] Richard J. Samuels, *The Business of the Japanese State, Energy Markets in Comparative and Historical Perspective*, Cornell University Press, Ithaca, 1987.

[26] Johnson, *MITI and the Japanese Miracle*, p. 49.

Amakudari, or 'the descent from heaven' is the practice of top bureaucrats moving out from their posts in order to allow younger colleagues their turn at the top of the extremely powerful bureaucracy by taking up posts in the private sector. As the term suggests, the private sector is less prestigious than the top civil service, in contrast to the situation in the United States. The extensive powers that the Japanese government has possessed for most of the modern era to steer economic growth through licences and the allocation of credit to key economic sectors, have made former bureaucrats with close ties to current civil servants valuable recruits. Indeed, at least until very recently, civil servants in Japan have been more powerful than the elected politicians who supposedly control the bureaucracy. Yet the practice should not be understood as it would be in the United States as being close to corruption warranting attempts by Congress to limit the recruitment of former top officials by companies they have dealt with and forbidding former officials to lobby their former agency for a set period. Amakudari, by placing top civil servants in key posts in business ties the state to business, but, given the loyalty of these former civil servants to their former careers, it also ties business to the state. The former civil servants retain the lifelong habits of respect for the policies and decisions of government, even if they now work for a private corporation.

Recruitment practices also tie the bureaucracy and business leaderships together. Being educated at Todai – the Tokyo Imperial University – is highly advantageous to those who wish to reach the top in either the civil service or big business. Former class mates retain even closer ties than exist among former public schoolboys in Britain or fraternity friends in the USA.

Finally, the Liberal Democratic Party, which has dominated Japanese politics forming all post-occupation governments, is highly dependent on big business for large-scale campaign contributions. Many former bureaucrats have also in retirement become LDP members of the Diet. Thus, while business and government are linked in spirit by a general tendency to see business and government as partners in growth, without any of the antagonism that characterizes the attitudes of American business executives to government, the relationship is also sustained by what Chalmers Johnson calls a 'skewed triangular relationship' between business, the LDP and the bureaucracy.

The LDP's role is to legitimate the decisions of the bureaucracy and to keep the bureaucracy within the limits the public will accept. The LDP staffs the bureaucracy with cadres to ensure it acts in line with what it thinks is good for the country. The business community supplies massive funds to keep the LDP in power – which however remains oriented upwards towards the bureaucracy rather than downward towards its main patrons.[27]

Not surprisingly, Johnson concludes that although there are disagreements between business and government, these disagreements are always 'among relatives'.[28]

In addition to all these advantages, the business community is extremely well organized. Individual industries are generally represented by trade associations employing high quality staff. Trade associations not only have ready access to government decisionmakers but, as in neocorporatist regimes, execute policy on behalf of government. 'Voluntary' export limitations (for example on the sale of cars to Britain and the USA) have been negotiated and implemented by trade associations. Industrial restructuring plans have been developed and implemented by trade associations, with the approval and assistance of the Ministry for International Trade and Industry (MITI). The trade associations are in turn members of the Keidanren, which has extremely close ties with MITI. MITI and the Keidanren are in constant contact with each other; indeed, the relationship between the two organizations is cemented by seconding staff to the Keidanren from MITI so that civil servants may better understand business's perspective on problems.

Several points of similarity exist between the situation in Japan and that in another practitioner of state-led growth, France. The truly extraordinary transformation of France between the end of the Second World War, when France was an economic laggard in Europe, and the 1980s, when France became an economic powerhouse of Europe with a gross national product per capita some 30 per cent higher than Britain's,[29] was an economic miracle more impressive than Germany's post-war recovery to a pre-eminence in the European economy interrupted only briefly by

[27] Ibid., p. 50.
[28] Ibid., p. 50.
[29] In 1988, Britain's GNP per capita was $9,616; France's GNP per capita was $13,077.

defeat in war. The French economic miracle was initiated and encouraged by the state through the mechanisms of the Five Year Plan and selective intervention in specific industries. Though the degree to which government could coerce industry into following the plans is debated, with Zysman emphasizing the state's influence over the allocation of credit[30] while older studies have asserted that government plans mattered little to industrial managers,[31] the state's concern to bring about a transformation of the French economy undoubtedly encouraged the building of ties with industry. The relative powerlessness of the politicians who made up the unstable governments of the Fourth Republic helped the planners in the state bureaucracy achieve a high degree of influence before the institutions of the Fifth Republic made an explicit transfer of power to the executive branch. Although 'cohabitation' within the executive between a prime minister of the right (Chirac) and a Socialist president (Mitterrand) caused some problems in the mid-1980s, power has remained within the executive branch throughout the Fifth Republic.

Like their Japanese counterparts, top civil servants in France have not in general displayed a high regard for interest groups. Interest groups have generally been seen as selfish factions which impede the pursuit of the general will, which is of course embodied by the state and in particular, senior civil servants. Yet the pursuit of economic growth required the building of bridges between the state and at least some sectors of industry. During the Fourth Republic, ties between government and particularly the more dynamic parts of industry were strengthened by the *Commissariat du Plan*, the agency charged with drawing up the Five Year Plan. Although a number of interests were supposedly consulted during the formulation of the plan, the process soon became in practice one which linked government and business. Certainly French unions, organizing only 20 per cent of the workforce into competing and conflicting Catholic, Communist and Socialist unions had nothing like the importance of employers.

At first, the links between business and government were not

---

[30] John Zysman, *Governments, Markets and Growth*, Cornell University Press, Ithaca and London, 1983.

[31] J. H. MacArthur and B. R. Scott, *Industrial Planning in France*, Harvard University Press, Cambridge, Mass., 1969.

so much based on links between business organizations and government as on links between government and specific companies. The major employers' organization, the Conseil National du Patronat Français (CNPF), was an insufficiently enthusiastic partner in the process of modernization, either opposing or accepting only sullenly most of the steps towards the creation of the European Community, for example. A variety of practices helped link government, particularly the civil service, to industry. The practice of amakudari finds its equivalent in *pantouflage*, the movement of formerly powerful and prestigious civil servants into key posts in industry. As in Japan, the top civil servants and officials of major companies frequently have a common educational background, this time in the Grandes Ecoles such as the Ecole Normale d'Administration or the Polytechnique which provide ties which last for life. Again as in Japan, former civil servants have been recruited into politics to serve in governing parties of the right, which have in turn been given significant campaign contributions by industry.

As time has passed, however, both business and government seem to have felt a need to develop a more institutionalized linkage. After the 'Events' of May 1968 prompted the Gaullist government to offer several major concessions to workers, employers decided on a thorough overhaul and strengthening of the CNPF. A long-standing tendency for small and medium-sized enterprises to decline in importance while large-scale enterprises gained, increased the power of those large enterprises within the CNPF; large enterprises were of course the companies most likely to be led by graduates of the Grandes Ecôles who favoured close partnership with the state.

Indeed, a recent study concludes that France has seen a trend towards neocorporatism in several sectors, even though the trend has not been of equal strength in all sectors of the economy.[32] It is perhaps in agriculture that the trend towards neocorporatism has been most dramatic. The Fédération Nationale des Syndicats

[32] John Keeler, *The Politics of Neocorporatism in France*, Oxford University Press, New York and Oxford, 1987. For another interpretation of the extent of neocorporatism in the French interest group system, see Frank L. Wilson, 'Interest groups and politics in western Europe: the neocorporatist approach', *Comparative Politics*, 16 (1982), pp. 105–23.

des Exploitants Agricoles (FNSEA) was transformed during the 1960s from being a pressure group engaged in confrontation with the state in the constant quest for higher agricultural prices into an interest group which welcomed partnership with the state in the quest for the modernization of French agriculture. The FNSEA gained obvious benefits from government in this partnership. Until the election of a Socialist government in 1981, which briefly attempted to halt the trend towards neocorporatism, the FNSEA enjoyed a privileged position, a monopoly more or less of representation for farmers and even government payments towards its expenses. In return, FNSEA provided not only technical advice and help in administration but also worked hard to damp down rural discontent even during times of hardship in the countryside. FNSEA's efforts to prevent violent protest in the countryside naturally prompted its critics to charge that it had become more concerned to keep its privileged ties to policymakers and government subsidies than to represent French farmers.

Unions have also been somewhat affected by a trend towards neocorporatism in the 1970s. Studies of French planning in the 1950s and 1960s concluded that the planning process was, in the words of Stephen Cohen, a 'partnership of big business, the state and in theory *though not in practice*, the trade unions'.[33] Of course, the Confédération Générale du Travail (CGT), the largest of the unions and dominated by the Communists, had withdrawn from the planning process in 1947 as the Cold War intensified. However, even the more moderate CFDT (Confédération Française Démocratique du Travail) and the relatively small Force Ouvrière had little impact on the planning process. The trend towards a somewhat greater involvement of unions in neocorporatism might be traced to the policy adopted in the early 1960s of the government paying subsidies to unions, perhaps to weaken the CGT by paying a higher proportion of the subsidies to the non-Communist unions than their memberships warranted. After the Events of May 1968, the trend towards incorporation of the unions intensified. The unions were involved in a tri-partite negotiation between the government, unions and employers to end the unrest of that eventful spring; thereafter, a number of tri-partite conferences were held on employment

[33] Stephen Cohen, *Modern Capitalist Planning, The French Model*, Harvard University Press, Cambridge, Mass., 1969, (emphasis added).

issues. Perhaps unsurprisingly, the Socialist government of 1981–6 consulted the unions more as part of its programme of democratizing the planning process. However, unions have still not enjoyed the status of the CNPF in the eyes of government officials. And ironically, as unions have come closer to being accepted as partners in the planning process, the process itself has diminished in importance. As France has become integrated into the European Community and, indeed, the international economy, the capacity of the French state to steer the economy through the *économie concertée* has diminished. In general, it can be concluded that for French unions, the trends towards neocorporatism were too little, too late.

France and Japan therefore remain as fascinating examples of uneven neocorporatism. The partnership between the state and employers is at least as close as that partnership is in countries which are accepted as fully neocorporatist. Yet unions are not fully integrated into the system. French unions, drawing on their capacity for occasional massive disruption (as in 1968) and the greatly increased political strength of the left in France in the 1980s have come somewhat closer to achieving equality of status with employers than have the Japanese without there being any real doubt, however, that they are still much inferior in status to employers. Whether or not it is reasonable to categorize France and Japan as countries which display 'corporatism without labour' or which should be regarded as constituting some separate form of relations between interest groups and the state is partly an heuristic question. For those who focus on unions, the temptation will be to exclude the two countries from the neocorporatist category. For those who want to focus on the integration of the state and interest groups, the tendency will be to include France and Japan in the neocorporatist group. It might be, however, that in both France and Japan, the state has been a more dominant partner than in most neocorporatist systems. The state has co-operated with business in France and Japan for its own purposes; de Gaulle promoted economic growth to enhance the prestige of France, not to please the business community. In contrast, the state is more of an equal or possibly even somewhat subservient partner in Sweden and Austria. Certainly the greater dominance of the state in France and Japan must make one wary of extending to them generalizations about neocorporatism.

5

Interests and States

We noted at the beginning of this book that the relationship between the state and major interests in society is or ought to be one of the major issues in political science. Until recently, discussion of this topic was constrained by the disappearance of the term 'state' from the discourse of political scientists. This disappearance was due to several factors. Political science in the 1950s and 1960s was concerned to be as 'scientific' as possible. Political commitment should be avoided, and, reflecting the influence of logical positivism, the work of political scientists either should be based on logical deduction or should be empirically falsifiable. In order to escape the emotive overtones and even mystical connotations of the word 'state', political scientists preferred to use phrases or words such as 'government' or 'political system'. In order to achieve a more manageable research agenda which was compatible with a positivist view of social science, political scientists focused their work on aspects or fragments of the state most readily observed, such as the behaviour of legislators, voters and, more rarely, judges and bureaucrats.

Several unfortunate consequences followed from the disappearance of the term 'state'. First, perhaps because of the popularity in the 1960s of the phrase 'the political system', policy was generally seen as the result of 'outside' forces such as interest groups or voters acting on the state. In spite of a large number of empirical works which we have encountered which pointed to the limited power of interest groups, the role of the state was generally seen as merely aggregating 'inputs' into public policy 'outputs'.[1] Only recently have we come to acknowledge more

---

[1] Gabriel Almond has recently attacked this interpretation, arguing that pluralist writers

readily the possibility that the agencies of the state can be autonomous actors.[2] Second, political science tended to fragment into disparate groups concerned with some aspect of the state, such as legislatures, courts or executives while the task of recombining the pieces into a picture of the whole was neglected. Third, political scientists tended to focus on the most obviously 'political' forms of behaviour, such as lobbying or voting, thus neglecting much, probably most, of the importance of the state. Most obviously, the bulk of the work of the state is not at any moment in time the subject of much political debate. The police arrest criminals, retirement pensions are paid and soldiers trained without voting behaviour, lobbying or other forms of political action being involved. More importantly, the neglect of the state resulted in an almost total neglect of the role of the state in *structuring* aspects of daily life from the most intimate (as in the definition of marriage and family relations) to the most commercial (such as which contracts can be enforced or what is the status of a joint stock corporation). Interest groups, organizations which are established and operate under rules established and enforced by the state, are particularly affected by this structuring characteristic of the state. Thus, one of the most exciting areas of political science for students of interest groups is the movement to 'bring the state back in'.[3]

Implicit Theories of Interest Groups and the State

Most writing relevant to the study of interest groups and the state, rarely addressing that relationship explicitly, was carried

---

did allow for autonomous action by government institutions. However, Eric Nordlinger provides a convincing argument that Almond exaggerates meagre hints in the literature that interest groups are not everything. For the exchange, see *American Political Science Review*, 82, 3, September 1988.

[2] Eric Nordlinger, *On the Autonomy of the Democratic State*, Harvard University Press, Cambridge, Mass., 1981.

[3] The phrase is of course Theda Skocpol's who has done so much to stimulate work in this area. Theda Skocpol, 'Bringing the state back in', in Peter Evans, Dietrich Rueschemeyer and Theda Skocpol, *Bringing the State Back In*, Cambridge University Press, Cambridge and New York, 1985. For an interesting response from the neocorporatist perspective see Philippe Schmitter, 'Neocorporatism and the state', in Wyn Grant (ed.), *The Political Economy of Corporatism*, Macmillan, Houndmills, 1985.

on in connection with either attacking or defending the pluralist or marxist traditions. Skocpol has argued interestingly that both pluralism and marxism misconstrue the nature of the state.

The majority of work on interest groups in Britain and the United States can be understood as an attempt to either support or attack pluralism. The debate has focused primarily, however, on whether or not interest groups do have more or less equal chances to form, gain access to decisionmakers and influence public policy. Pluralists, as we have seen, argued that power was widely dispersed and that many groups had a significant opportunity to influence public policy. This is not to say that *all* groups had an equal opportunity to influence public policy or that all groups had equal resources; such a claim, often attributed to pluralists by their critics, would have been manifestly absurd. Differences of income, status, size and quality of staffs and electoral significance obviously distinguish some interest groups from others. Yet clearly there was considerable room for debate about whether or not the interest group system gave most interest groups a more or less equal chance to influence policy, or whether it in fact gave wildly disproportionate power to relatively few interests. A number of participants in the debate, such as Dahl himself and Lindblom, clearly changed their opinion somewhat on this subject as time passed.[4]

From the perspective of the relationship of interest groups to the state, however, the debate on the degree of equality or inequality among interest groups is of secondary importance. For those who wish 'to bring the state back in', the problem with the debate over the pluralist approach to interest groups is not the conclusion that interest groups are more or less equal, but the belief that interest groups are organizations which can be separated from the state, that interest groups are spontaneously created, autonomous organizations 'outside' the state exerting successful 'pressure' on it. This belief, which can be held both by pluralists and their critics, in the view of the 'statist' writers, fundamentally

---

[4] For a history of the debate over pluralism, see G. David Garson, *Group Theories of Politics*, Sage Publications, Beverly Hills, 1978. For the major works on pluralism, see ch. 1. For the works of the older Dahl and Lindblom retreating from their fully pluralist positions of earlier years, see Robert Dahl, *Dilemmas of Pluralist Democracy*, Yale University Press, New Haven, 1982, esp. ch. 3; Charles E. Lindblom, *Politics and Markets, the World's Political Economic Systems*, Basic Books, New York, 1977.

misconstrues the relationship between states and interest groups. Pluralists and their critics make two errors, in the view of state theorists. First, because of their 'society centred'[5] view of the world, pluralists and their critics attribute too much power to interest groups. As Nordlinger argues, states can act autonomously, i.e., independently of the wishes of *any* interest group, or can act in alliance with some interests and against others, choosing allies to suit the purposes of the state.[6] Second, the state itself actually shapes the interest group system, directly contrary to the assumption made by both pluralists and their critics that interest groups are autonomous actors.

How do states influence the interest group system? There are in fact many different ways. The first way is the constitutional and legal environment which the state provides. Stepan has argued that the Anglo-American democracies with their common law tradition are significantly different from the countries influenced by the Roman law tradition.[7] The Anglo-American tradition has assumed the autonomy and spontaneity of interest groups. Interest groups are the result of spontaneous, voluntary activity. In contrast, in countries with Roman law traditions, interest groups are seen as being authorized and licensed by the state. Although in the twentieth century regulation of the affairs of certain types of interest groups, such as unions and corporations, has become extensive, in general the legal and constitutional traditions of the United States and Britain have assumed that interest groups should be left alone as much as possible. The constitutional guarantees of freedom of assembly to petition government have been particularly effective in this regard. As we have noted, attempts by southern states in the 1950s to force the National Association for the Advancement of Colored People (NAACP) to publish its membership lists were invalidated by the Supreme Court as infringing on these basic constitutional guarantees. The Supreme Court has also held sacrosanct the right of interest groups to communicate with their members freely even when in so doing they open a major loophole in laws regulating election

---

[5] Again, the phrase is Skocpol's, 'Bringing the state back in'.

[6] Nordlinger, *On the Autonomy of the Democratic State.*

[7] Alfred Stepan, *State and Society, Peru in Comparative Perspective,* Princeton University Press, Princeton, 1978.

campaign finance, and when, in the case of electricity generating companies, the right is used to urge support for nuclear power.

The legal and constitutional framework is relevant in another respect. The capacity of the state to shape interest groups is closely related to the structure of the state itself. In centralized states in which power is concentrated in the executive, the ability of the policymakers to restrict access to relatively few, favoured groups is high. As has been emphasized repeatedly above, the ability to control access to policymakers has been used in a variety of countries to encourage interest groups to merge or to show more responsibility in their attitudes. Thus, in both Britain and France, the leading farmers' organizations (the National Farmers' Union and FNSEA) were protected from competitors, by policymakers refusing to talk to their competitors, in return for realism and moderation. In states such as the USA in which power is dispersed among competing institutions, the capacity to control interest group access to policymakers is low. An interest group out of favour with a Republican administration in the White House may well find that for much the same reasons it is very much in favour with liberal Democrats in Congress. Interest groups without much influence in either the executive branch or Congress may find, as did the NAACP in the 1950s, that they can prevail in the courts. The ability of the state to shape either the attitudes or the structure of interest groups is reduced because the state itself lacks the capacity for co-ordinated action towards interest groups.

A wide variety of states do, however, try to shape the interest group system. Thus, even in the United States, where the expectation that the state should shape interest groups is lowest, administrations and Congress have in fact often exerted a significant influence on the interest group system. President Taft encouraged the creation of the Chamber of Commerce. The National Rifle Association was fostered by government (e.g., through supplying weapons) in order to increase the supply of trained marksmen in the event of war. The American Farm Bureau Federation was encouraged by government agricultural advisers (County Extension Agents) both to help with their work and to forestall the establishment of more radical farm organizations. The American Medical Association was immensely strengthened by the fact that it was necessary until recently in many states to join the AMA to be licensed to practise medicine. Similarly, British governments have sometimes encouraged the development of particular interest groups. The major employers' organization, the Confederation of British Industries, was brought into existence at the urging of the 1964–70 Labour government which needed a unified employers' organization which could participate in the indicative economic planning then in vogue.

Governments also subsidize interest groups which conform to their expectations. We have encountered earlier the French system of paying subsidies to a variety of interest groups in such a way that the government could particularly help its favoured interest groups. Yet even in the United States, the Reagan administration found to its surprise that it was subsidizing many interest groups critical of its policies which received grants for a variety of purposes (such as training) from different government agencies. The administration launched an only partially successful drive to 'defund the left' by denying liberal interest groups government grants and contracts. It is perhaps more common for interest groups to be subsidized indirectly through the granting of tax concessions to those which conform to some standard. In the United States, for example, interest groups which eschew directly political activity (as opposed to 'educational' endeavours) have been given a status by the Internal Revenue Service (IRS) which not only protects them from paying tax but which allows taxpayers to reduce their tax liability by making contributions to the interest group. If the interest group functions as an educational charity in the view of the IRS, contributions to it are an expenditure which can be set against tax. If the interest group is not a charity, this happy state of affairs does not apply. The question of where the line between political and educational work should be drawn is of course controversial, and both the Nixon and Reagan administrations sought to weaken their environmentalist critics by defining political activities more broadly and tax exempt activities more narrowly.

Laws may make it more or less difficult for interest groups to form. The United States again provides interesting examples of how states may help and hinder interest group formation. After a long period in which governments in the United States used police and troops to hinder attempts to form unions, the 1936 Wagner Act placed the weight of the federal government behind such attempts. Employees were given the right to hold a ballot to see if they wished to be represented by a union. If a majority voted in favour, the employer was obliged by federal law to recognize the union and bargain with it in good faith. The 1947 Taft–Hartley Act brought about several changes which made union organizing more difficult by forbidding secondary activities (i.e., strikes by workers not directly involved) and by allowing states to pass 'right to work' laws making closed shops illegal. The alleged bias of the body which enforces federal labour law, the National Labor Relations Board (NLRB), against unions and in favour of employers has been seen as one of the causes of the precipitous decline in the strength of unions in the United States.[8] It is also often argued, as we have seen, that the weakness of trade associations in the United States is due to fear that closer co-operation between employers would contravene the anti-monopoly statutes, which are stricter in the USA than in Britain. Similar stories could be told of how the state in other countries has fostered or hindered the growth of interest groups.

Governments have also attempted to shape interest groups through dubious or illegal means. The COINTELPRO programme of the Federal Bureau of Investigation (FBI) was designed to disrupt radical groups campaigning against American involvement in the Vietnam War. This flagrantly unconstitutional behaviour was repeated in the 1980s when an FBI investigation, of whether or not a group opposed to administration policy in Central America (CISPES) was itself breaking the law, degenerated into unconstitutional and illegal attempts to harass the organization. The placing of a bomb aboard the Greenpeace ship, *Rainbow Warrior* by French intelligence agents (murdering one person on board) might also serve as an example of the unorthodox approaches states sometimes adopt to interest group activities.

It would be perverse, therefore, to deny that the state is anything other than a powerful influence on the structure of the interest group system. Yet it would be equally perverse to deny that other factors are involved over which the state has little control. Class consciousness or the lack of it will influence significantly the

---

[8] For an interesting discussion of the recent history of the NLRB, see Terry Moe, 'Interests, institutions and positive theory: the NLRB', in *Studies in American Political Development*, 2, pp. 236–302, Yale University Press, New Haven, 1988.

proportion of workers prepared to join unions and, as employers' organizations have often developed in response to the development of unions, the degree of class consciousness indirectly influences the development of employers' organizations. The strength of employers' organizations and unions may also influence the degree to which other interest groups, such as farmers, feel obligated to organize to defend their interests. Political cultures, the prevailing patterns of beliefs about politics and government, also have a substantial impact on interest groups. In some countries, functional representation, the representation of individuals by groups representing occupational groupings in society, has a history reaching back to the Middle Ages. In other countries, such as the United States, occupational groups are often attacked as 'special interest groups' whose illegitimate influence weakens the position of the legitimate, elected representatives of the people. Finally, as those following such rational choice theorists as Olson, James Q. Wilson or Moe have emphasized,[9] interest groups may gain strength because they meet a variety of needs which are quite independent of their policy concerns. Interest groups may gain membership through providing cheap insurance, the use of grain elevators, companionship, the pleasure of being with like-minded people or even simply the psychological rewards of having made a commitment by joining as well as representation.

States, then, are not free to shape interest group systems as they wish. There are other important influences. Nor, as we have seen, are all states equally capable by virtue of their own design to shape their interest group systems. The highly fragmented American state is inherently less capable of influencing the interest group system than more cohesive and unified states such as France (at least at the high point of the Fifth Republic). Yet even the American state, as we have seen, has a certain degree of power to influence the interest group system helping or retarding social forces strengthening or weakening an interest such as labour. It follows that there exist opportunities for a statecraft of interest groups through which the state may, if so minded, use its resources

[9] Mancur Olson, *The Logic of Collective Action: Public Goods and the Theory of Groups*, Schocken Books, New York, 1968; James Q. Wilson, *Political Organizations*, Basic Books, New York, 1974; Terry Moe, *The Organization of Interests*, University of Chicago Press, Chicago, 1980.

to influence the relative power of different interests (e.g., labour and management) or to help shape the overall structure of the interest group system. States can, to some degree, shape interest groups.

Marxist Theory and Interest Groups

This is not the place to attempt an overall evaluation of marxism. Yet it is clear that until very recently marxist writings had very little to contribute to the study of interest groups. For the most common view of the state in marxist writings until recently assumed a most unconvincing (to non-marxists) uniformity among states, so that the basic character and functions of all were identical.[10]

It may well be, as Badie and Birnbaum have argued,[11] that Marx himself was aware of the surely unstartling fact that there are significant differences between states, so that the state in mid-nineteenth century Prussia or Russia was radically different from the state in the same period in England or the United States. Yet the other interpretation of the state to be found in Marx's writings, the view of the state as 'but the executive committee of the bourgeoisie' long dominated marxist theory. States were mere epiphenomena, their nature determined by the property relationships within their societies, whose purposes were simply to guard property rights through mystification, repression and a small measure of amelioration of the worst consequences of capitalism.

The growth of the modern welfare state has made it hard for all but the most dogmatic to argue that the state does nothing for the working class but repress it.[12] The provision of education, pensions, health care and other welfare state services to working

[10] For most valuable discussions of the marxist theory of the state, see Bob Jessop, 'Recent theories of the capitalist state', *Cambridge Journal of Economics*, 1 (1977), pp. 353–73 and Jessop's *The Capitalist State: Theory and Methods*, New York University Press, New York, 1982. See also Martin Carnoy, *The State and Political Theory*, Princeton University Press, Princeton, 1984.

[11] Bertrand Badie and Pierre Birnbaum, *The Sociology of the State*, University of Chicago Press, Chicago, 1983.

[12] Such a view does however seem to be expressed by James O'Connor, *The Fiscal Crisis of the State*, St Martin's Press, New York, 1971.

people may not be perfect, but far outstrips anything which Marx could have imagined. Sophisticated marxists no longer assume a uniformity of interest among capitalists but realize that capitalists are divided into different, sometimes conflicting, groups, a discovery made long ago by other social scientists. Marxist scholars have also become more aware of the variety of relationships which exist in capitalist societies between different industrial sectors, finance and the state. Instead of assuming that all capitalist countries are more or less the same, marxist writers now appreciate that there are very significant differences between Japan and the United States, or between West Germany and Britain in the linkages between different capitalist groups (e.g., manufacturers and financiers) and such groups and the state. Finally, in an era when the state in several countries disposes of well over half the gross national product (and when the OECD average for government expenditures as a percentage of GNP is 44 per cent), it has become difficult to treat the state as a mere adjunct of capitalist society. The state has often been seen as an alternative allocator of resources to the market; the trend in history has been fairly clearly (even in the United States) for the state rather than the market to allocate a larger and larger proportion of society's resources.

In short, the state and its relations with major interests in society have become as problematic for marxist as for non-marxist writers. The state is no longer viewed simply as the servant of a unified bourgeoisie. Other interest groups, such as unions, may be able to make important 'gains' through playing what would once have been decried as the bourgeois political game. Yet if the state is not merely the servant of certain interests (that is, for marxists, the capitalists), what is it? Under what circumstances and to what extent can the state act against the interests of capitalists and in alliance with other interests?

Marxist theory no longer generates a simplification about the role of the state, but like 'bourgeois' social science, a research agenda. Moreover, in some respects the research agendas of different traditions seem to have converged in response to what writers from a variety of backgrounds thought to be a 'crisis of the state'.

The State Overwhelmed?

The convergence between marxists and non-marxists was evident in the literature which arose in the late 1970s on the overwhelming of the state by interest groups. Political science, for better or worse, is responsive to current events, and current events in the 1960s and 1970s seemed to suggest that interest groups had increased in power *vis-à-vis* the state. Writers in the pluralist tradition such as Beer, King, Rose and Peters have suggested that the 1970s witnessed a crisis of governability during which interest groups made greater and more varied claims on the state, which the state was less and less able to satisfy.[13] The traditional claims for subsidies for farmers, development grants for business and increased legal powers for unions were joined by demands from public interest groups for a clean environment, enhanced consumer protection and political reform. One perceptive study of American interest groups noted that there had been an 'interest group explosion' with many more interest groups than previously opening offices in Washington and establishing political action committees.[14] Others noted that business, regarded by Lindblom as so privileged that it scarcely needed to rely on conventional interest group tactics, was energetically improving the quantity and quality of its representation in Washington.[15]

Neo-marxists refer to these developments as a 'legitimation crisis'.[16] The state was experiencing greater and greater difficulty in legitimating the capitalist system in the face of rising expectations. As Birch has noted,[17] some of the language used by neo-marxists such as Habermas has an almost neo-conservative

---

[13] Samuel Beer, *Britain Against Itself*, W. W. Norton, New York, 1982: Anthony King (ed.) *Why is Britain Becoming Harder to Govern?*, BBC Publications, London, 1976; Richard Rose and B. Guy Peters, *Can Government Go Bankrupt?*, Basic Books, New York, 1978.

[14] Jeffrey Berry, *The Interest Group Society*, Little Brown, Boston, 1984.

[15] Graham K. Wilson, *Interest Groups in the United States*, Oxford University Press, Oxford, 1981, ch. 4; David Vogel, 'The power of business in the United States, a reappraisal', *BJPolS*, 13 (1983), pp. 385–408.

[16] Jurgen Habermas, *Legitimation Crisis*, tr. Thomas McCarthy, Beacon Press, Boston, 1975.

[17] Anthony Birch, 'Overload, ungovernability and delegitimation', *BJPolS*, 14 (1984), pp. 135–60.

character, as when Habermas compares citizens of welfare states to factory farm chickens. James O'Connor, another neo-marxist writer, agrees with neo-conservatives that the state is being overloaded although he sees the increased expectations stemming not so much from popular demands on governments as from the needs of capitalists to reduce their costs by transferring as much as possible of these costs to government in order to protect profits. Thus employers seek not only to maintain the quantity and quality of their labour force through state welfare and education policies but also try to have the state pay for research and development costs through military expenditures.[18] (It is interesting to note that President Reagan's Star Wars initiative has often been seen as an 'industrial policy of the right' promoting government-financed research on projects such as super-computers under the banner of military expenditure.)

The politics of the 1980s cast doubt on the overload idea. Governments such as Thatcher's in Britain, Reagan's in America and centre–right coalitions in countries such as the Netherlands not only refused additional demands on the state (e.g., for increased subsidies from coal miners in Britain) but even refused to meet long-established expectations (e.g., that full employment would be maintained). Both Britain and the United States, often used as examples in the overload literature, witnessed some contraction of the involvement of the state in social and economic life, partially obscured by a dramatic increase in spending on the military and police. Governments in many western countries rediscovered the fact that in the words of anti-drug abuse commercials of the 1980s they could 'Just Say "No"' to interest group demands.

What, if anything, had been mistaken in the overload literature? First, many of the apparent weaknesses of the state had been brought about not by popular demand but by mistaken initiatives by the state itself. Frequently the state was weakened by 'over-reach' not 'overload'. Thus the problems of governance in the United States were increased dramatically by the Vietnam War, which though supported by large sectors of public opinion throughout the 1960s, was brought about by presidential initiative rather than public clamour. Similarly, incomes policies in Britain,

[18] O'Connor, *The Fiscal Crisis of the State.*

which led to the confrontation with the miners which Heath lost in 1974, were due not so much to their initial popularity with the public as to the belief amongst policymakers that incomes policies would allow the maintenance of full employment without inflation. The attempt to control the rate of increase of wages in every industrial sector extended the power of the state to a degree to which it had never stretched before.

Second, overload theorists exaggerated the degree of change in popular opinion. Opinion poll evidence does not suggest that ordinary voters expected more from government in the 1970s, whatever the leaders of interest groups said. On the contrary, the public looked sceptically and cautiously at the power of government to satisfy their needs. In the United States, for example, the 1970s witnessed a dramatic decline in confidence in the ability and integrity of federal government, a decline which began before Watergate, though that even did little to reverse the trend. The election of a Democrat, Jimmy Carter, who ran against Washington in 1976 and that of a conservative Republican, Ronald Reagan, in 1980 were perhaps expressions of this anti-government sentiment.

Third, states proved to have more resilience in facing interest group demands than anticipated. No interest groups discovered this more painfully than unions. In the United States, the Reagan administration destroyed the seemingly strategically-placed air traffic controllers' union, PATCO, when it called a strike in contravention of federal law. The coalminers in Britain, who had humbled Edward Heath, met their match in Margaret Thatcher. Thatcher showed that the state possessed reserve powers in terms of the deployment of police and the discovery of hitherto unsuspected legal powers (e.g., to stop people intending to join picket lines hundreds of miles away) with which to answer the miners' tactics of massive, coercive picketing. In 1972, the Yorkshire miners' leader, Arthur Scargill had used mass pickets to blockade a coke depot at Saltley thus making the miners' strike extremely effective and had subsequently boasted of the value of this unlawful action; in 1984–5, the government organized nationally for the first time sufficient concentrations of police to prevent a repetition of the tactic. Whether this change should be seen as due mainly to a learning process through which the state learned better how to confront challenges to its authority (and of course police technology for dealing with riots had improved considerably throughout the 1970s and early 1980s) or to Thatcher herself having greater resolve than Heath is unclear.

Fourth, the surprising resilience of classic liberal economic thought provided states with both an intellectual escape route and a means of legitimating their escape from confines, particularly the commitment to full employment, which had made them dependent on the co-operation of interest groups to operate policies such as incomes restraint. The belief that governments could guarantee full employment had never been fully accepted in the United States, where as late as the early 1970s President Nixon could announce to the surprise of many that he had been converted to Keynesianism. Many of his Republican colleagues did not share his economic conversion and by the end of the 1970s, the rise of monetarism had placed Keynesian economists on the defensive. More surprising, perhaps, was the success of neo-liberal economic doctrine in Keynes's own country, Britain. Doubts had been increasing in academic and policymaking circles about the feasibility of government stabilization of the economy throughout the 1970s. Mrs Thatcher's homely comparisons between domestic and national economics though mocked by many intellectuals also proved to have popular appeal.

In any event, the return to popularity of a more liberal, less interventionist approach to economic policymaking had profound consequences for the relationship between government and organized interests. Once the commitment to full employment was ended, the need to secure the co-operation of employers and unions in tri-partite incomes policies was ended. Once the belief that detailed government intervention in specific industries would promote economic growth was abandoned, so too could the need for close co-operation with trade associations, unions and general employers' organizations be abandoned. Thus the Confederation of British Industries as well as the Trades Union Congress found that their status was much reduced during the Thatcher years. In the United States, the free market policies of the Reagan administration similarly halted the trend in the 1970s for employers' organizations to be strengthened; the need for stronger employers' organizations to be developed to curtail government interference had vanished. Although individual corporations remained politically active, they were frequently to be found on opposite sides of the question so that their influence cancelled out. For example, a far more sweeping set of tax reforms was enacted in 1986 than political scientists had predicted in part because pressure from corporations which would benefit cancelled out pressure from corporations which would lose, leaving politicians a freer choice than had been expected. Thus the apparent weakening of the state as it retreated from responsibilities such as securing full employment in fact served to strengthen the state *vis-à-vis* interest groups on which the state became less dependent.

Of course, not all countries were as drawn as were Britain and the United States to neo-liberal experiments. Although, as we have seen, the neocorporatist regimes experienced what by their standards was a period of instability, the fundamental features of neocorporatism have survived. Indeed, the admirers of neo-corporatist regimes such as Schmitter have argued, as we noted above, that the more neocorporatist was a country, the better it survived shocks to the international economic order which occurred in the 1970s and 1980s. Inflation, unemployment and government deficits were all better contained by the more neocorporatist countries. Neocorporatism not only made the economic train run on time but constituted an effective, less painful method than the neo-liberal approaches of Britain and the United States to the problems of overload. Neocorporatism solved through consensus the problems that might result from powerful interest groups, whereas Britain and the United States waged costly struggles to weaken groups, particularly, though not exclusively, unions. Neocorporatism might therefore be a superior solution to the crisis of the state on both efficiency and normative grounds. Yet is the normative superiority of neocorporatism so clear?

It is clear that behind the discussions of the advantages of neocorporatism lurk important normative questions. Defenders of neocorporatism can argue not only that neocorporatist arrangements promote efficiency (a claim which in any case, as we have seen, is less obviously true in the 1980s than the 1970s) but that it constitutes a form of negotiated capitalism in which the interests of the less advantaged are better protected than in market systems. Neocorporatist bargaining will promote the development of welfare states of particular value to the less wealthy; it will also facilitate the maintenance of full employment, with obvious advantages for wage earners. Finally, neocorporatism brings within the framework of negotiation by politicians and interest group leaders questions which otherwise would be left to the workings of blind market forces.

Yet there is also a normative case to be made against neocorporatism. In the first place, neocorporatism necessarily grants significant power to interest groups, power which extends beyond their immediate area of interest. Such influence may, or may not, be exercised in accordance with the values of interest group members. Although unions, for example, in neocorporatist countries have an impressive density of membership (i.e., recruitment of a very high proportion of potential members), there is no reason to suppose that they have been more successful than unions elsewhere in fostering effective internal democracy. Further, the power enjoyed by interest groups in neocorporatist systems implies a reduction in the influence of elected politicians, who, for all their imperfections, are indeed responsible and often responsive to the electorate. Finally, neocorporatist systems link a relatively small number and range of interest groups to policymakers. Certainly employers' organizations and unions have effective input to policymaking. What opportunities exist for women's groups, environmentalists or representatives of immigrants to obtain access through the neocorporatist system? The social democratic traditions of unions in neocorporatist systems mean that unions are more likely to be concerned about many of these interests than would, for example, craft unions in the United States. Yet it would be unrealistic to expect even the most politically conscious unions to subordinate traditional concerns with full employment, wages and benefits to a 'new politics' concern such as protecting the environment.

It is striking how little most writers on neocorporatism have been concerned by normative concerns which have been such a central element in the critique of pluralism. No doubt this lack of concern is due in part to a feeling that the partnership of labour with government and business in administering the economy marks a significant extension of democracy compared with the situation in countries in which the workings of the economy are left to market forces alone. Neocorporatism allows representatives of workers to participate in the making of choices such as the trade-off between inflation and unemployment which in other countries are merely imposed on them. Yet it is hard to avoid the feeling that the main concern of those writing on neocorporatism has been not to evaluate it as a system of representation but to show that neocorporatism as a form of 'organized capitalism' has been more *efficient* than more market-oriented economic systems. Writers such as Schmitter have generally been concerned to show not that neocorporatism improves the representativeness of political systems but that it reduces the risk of undesirable developments such as inflation, unemployment or low economic growth. Whether or not this claim is true is debatable. It is strikingly different, however, from the claims that are made about the advantages or disadvantages of pluralism, which are nearly always couched in terms of the impact of pluralism on the quality of representation in the political system.

Neocorporatism therefore represents a way in which the pressures of interests on the state can be managed. In pluralist interest group systems, either the state would be protected by the tendency of numerous competing interest groups to weaken each other, so that as Madison had hoped in *Federalist No. 10*, faction would constrain faction, or, as the overload theorists had feared, the state would buckle as numerous interest groups each demanded a pay-off. Neocorporatism offered alternative means of reducing the burden of interest group demands. The granting of monopolies by the state for representation to relatively few interest groups would give the state some leverage, encouraging moderation on the part of interest groups in return for access to policymakers. The partnership of interest groups in governing would encourage an awareness among interest group leaders of the real constraints under which government worked. Finally, neocorporatist interest groups could make sacrifices to the common welfare without fear of competitors refusing to make similar concessions.

As we have seen, there is disagreement about the extent to which neocorporatism is a system which can be exported and the degree to which it emerges 'naturally' in a limited number of states or industrial sectors. Most would agree, however, that even if state encouragement is not a sufficient condition for the existence of neocorporatism it is a necessary condition. Neocorporatism will not emerge or persist unless the state encourages it. Only the state can supply the willingness to take interest groups into partnership with policymakers and the building up of the stature of the 'social partners' by refusing to consult as closely with rival interest groups. Neocorporatism is therefore a step away from the idea of interest group systems found in pluralism as something which the state is powerless to affect, though for their part interest groups may have a major impact on the state. In neocorporatist systems, the state has to accept certain facts which are the result of social forces it cannot fully control (such as the strength of unions in Sweden or Austria) but it then manipulates those facts to avoid the dangers of excessive interest group power.

In some cases, states have been freer to manipulate the interest group system to serve their own purposes. France perhaps supplies the classic example. The senior civil servants and politicians managing the brilliant drive for modernization and industrial growth in France have taken different groups into partnership as they have in their turn served the interests of the state. The encouragement of the Jeunes Agricoles to take over and operate the main agricultural interest group, the FNSEA in partnership with the state in modernizing agriculture is a case in point. Perhaps even more important was the relationship between the state and the more dynamic parts of French manufacturing industry, a relationship managed first through direct contacts between officials and major corporations, then through the CNPF, whose strengthening and modernization had been encouraged by the state. Even the comparative strength of different unions was influenced to an important degree by the granting of disproportionately large subsidies to more moderate unions. In short, in pluralism the state is seen as the helpless victim of interest groups, unless interest groups hold each other in check. In neocorporatist systems, the state manipulates its interest group environment by taking some interest groups into particularly close partnership, but is also forced itself to come to terms with the fact that like it or not, certain interests are too powerful to ignore. Finally, in other states such as France and Japan, the state actively promotes those interest groups which will serve the interests and policies of the state.

Interest Group or State Power?

Whatever the configuration of the relationship between the state and interest groups, be it the integration of neocorporatism or the distance of more pluralist arrangements, we shall be left with the classic question of 'who gets what' from the relationship? Unfortunately, it may well be impossible to generalize. Lowi has led the way in reminding us that policy areas differ in their politics; so, therefore, does the power of interest groups. Interest groups in any country may have significant influence in one area (e.g., the regulation of important utilities and industries) while having less influence in other areas (e.g., foreign policy). Yet it is clear that the power of interest groups in a particular policy area (such as industrial policy) also varies from one country to another, as does the power or relative autonomy of the state. In some countries, government assistance to industry has been given for purposive reasons of national policy, whereas in other countries (such as the USA or Britain), government assistance to industry has been given primarily to ease the complaints of industries which are in difficulty. Thus, the power of interest groups over the state is a function not only of the policy area under discussion but of the general power or autonomy of the state itself.

This is not the place to begin an extended discussion of what influences the character of states. Numerous factors play a part. Long-standing cultural attitudes towards authority in general and the power of the state in particular clearly play a part, as one has only to compare Japan and the USA to see. The location of the state throughout its history both in terms of its vulnerability to military attack and its position as a leader or follower in international economic development is also relevant. States which are militarily vulnerable or which have had to 'catch up' economically have generally accumulated more power from their citizens than those which have not. The organization of the state itself is important; is there a prestigious, cohesive bureaucracy, or not? Is the state organized into relatively cohesive institutions, or, like the USA into overlapping and competing institutions? These, and many other questions determine the nature of the state that interest groups confront.

Yet if there can be no safe generalizations about the relative power of interest groups and the states which encompass them, we can at least, on the basis of the earlier descriptive chapters, lay to rest some myths. For example, the visibility of interest groups is no guarantee of their importance. The highly visible interest groups of the USA play a less interesting role in the governance of their country than do the much less visible interest groups of the neocorporatist countries. More important is the fact that well-organized interest groups are not necessarily associated with weak states. On the contrary, some of the most impressive looking interest groups exist in countries with strong looking states. The Keidanren in Japan, for example, is more impressive in terms of its authority, staff and comprehensiveness of membership than any of the competing organizations which claim to speak for American employers. Yet few would deny that the Japanese state is more powerful or autonomous than the American.

Indeed, well-organized interest groups, which, as the overload theorists noted, are a potential threat to weak states, can be a considerable help to strong states. Political scientists have long noted the help that interest groups can give to policymakers. Interest groups warn of both political and practical disadvantages which might follow adoption of policy proposals. In today's increasingly complex societies, state bureaucracies rarely possess the knowledge necessary to forecast accurately the consequences of most policy proposals. Interest groups are in short part of the nerves of government, keeping policymakers in touch with the realities of the world.

Strong interest groups also aid the state in policy implementation. Competing, fragmented interest groups cannot take over the implementation of policy as readily as can unified interest groups whose legitimacy is greater and whose fear of losing members by taking some unpopular decisions is less than for fragmented, competing interest groups. Regulatory policy provides an interesting example. The stronger interest groups of Britain were able to take over the formulation of regulations dealing with contentious issues such as occupational safety and health whereas the same issue became a nightmare for the relevant agency in the USA. The interest groups of neocorporatist countries such as Sweden have in turn implemented policies such as incomes restraint which overwhelmed the British state. Yet such a helpful role for interest groups can more probably be achieved when the state retains a plausible capacity to act if interest groups will not help. Interest groups are most likely to help in implementing policies when they know that a less welcome alternative could be produced if they withdraw co-operation. British interest groups are more likely to help in implementing regulatory policy than American groups not because they are more statesman-like than their American counterparts but because they know that if they do not help, the state may act without their help and contrary to their wishes.[19] The fear of state action induces interest group co-operation without which life in turn would be more difficult for the state.

Indeed, strong states and strong interest groups might be mutually supportive. Just as strong interest groups can strengthen the state by relieving it of troublesome political issues, so the strong state might encourage the development of strong interest groups. Such encouragement might occur not only because of the policies and unintended consequences of state action described above but because of the consequences of perceptions of the state itself. In general, the more likely it is that action will significantly affect people or interests, the more likely it is that strong interest groups will form to protect those people or interests who possess the resources to do so. As we have seen, when the American state seemed unlikely to cause any problems for business in the 1950s, business organizations were weak. As the 'threat' to business rose in the 1960s and 1970s, business organizations were strengthened. It is scarcely surprising that some of the strongest interest groups in the world are in countries where the state is strongest in terms of the range and scale of activities it undertakes. Swedish interest groups, as we have seen, are in general stronger than American; the Swedish state plays a much more extensive role in its society than does the American state in the USA. Strong states encourage the creation of strong interest groups.

---

[19] See David Vogel, *National Styles of Regulation*, Cornell University Press, Ithaca, 1986.

Conclusions

States are not merely recipients of interest group pressure. States can act autonomously of all interest groups, or work in alliance with some interest groups against others. States also, within limits, create and shape both interest groups and interest group systems. We have tried to delineate some of the conditions under which states are more or less able to shape interest group systems to their own liking. Even when states do not, or cannot act consciously to shape interest group systems, however, the character of the state still exerts a profound effect on the nature of the interest group system. This in turn raises the question of what shapes the character of states. That, however, is a profoundly complicated question, which we are fortunate to be able to leave to others.

6

Interest Groups and Political Parties

Interest groups and political parties are often seen as rivals. Both provide avenues for political participation and claim to be effective methods for influencing public policy. The money or energy which citizens devote to interest groups might in principle be made available instead to political parties. Indeed, political parties and interest groups are often seen not only as competitors for limited political resources, but as antipathetic to each other's power.[1] When political parties are strong, it is argued, interest groups are weakened; when interest groups are strong, political parties are weakened. This maxim, popular with political scientists who study differences in the politics of the American states,[2] is based on the supposed integrative character of political parties, which it is argued must appeal to numerous different groups in order to win elections, and the alleged disintegrative nature of interest groups, which speak for smaller sectors of society. No political party can win a majority by being identified with a single interest. As Schattschneider wrote in criticizing earlier writing:

The notion that political parties are aggregates of special interest groups held together by an endless process of negotiation and concession is unrealistic .... It underestimates the fact that we have a two party system. *The parties compete with each other*; they do not compete with pressure groups. The amount of bargaining they have to do with special interest groups is limited by the fact that each party must cope primarily

[1] E. E. Schattschneider, *The Semi-Sovereign People: A Realist's View of Democracy*, Holt, Reinhart and Winston, New York, 1960.
[2] L. Harman Zeigler, 'Interest groups in the American states', in Virginia Gray, Herbert Jacobs and Kenneth Vines (eds), *Politics in the American States*, Little Brown, Boston, 1983, pp. 97–131.

with its *party* opposition. Neither party can afford to make excessive concessions to any pressure group.[3]

Moreover, in states or countries with strong political parties, party discipline will constrain and offset pressure from localized interests in legislators' districts. To the degree that political parties stress political principles or issues which affect the nation as a whole, they provide an antidote to excessive interest group power. V. O. Key had concluded in his magisterial survey of politics in the old South that the absence of strong, competitive parties produced politics dominated by factions, individuals and interests.[4]

The belief that strong parties and strong interest groups are incompatible is deeply rooted, therefore, in political science. Yet this assumption, though not without empirical support, seems in conflict with experience outside the United States. We shall see that the relationship between political parties and interest groups is much more complicated than any unqualified assertion that strong interest groups and strong parties cannot coexist allows.

How clearly can we distinguish the roles of interest groups and political parties? The conventional distinction drawn between interest groups and political parties is that interest groups can be distinguished from political parties in terms of the nature and range of their activities. Interest groups seek to influence government without taking over its administration and are concerned with relatively few, focused concerns. Political parties in contrast nominate candidates for office and are concerned with a wide variety of issues.

It is not so clear in fact that interest groups do not try to take over aspects of government. Much of the literature on interest groups stresses the blurring of lines or functions between interest groups and government. Part of the idea of an 'issue network' is that boundaries between government and interest groups can be less important than boundaries between different policy communities. The central concern of neocorporatist writing was to show that interest groups were partners of government in both the formulation and implementation of policy. Interest groups

---

[3] Schattschneider, *The Semi-Sovereign People*, p. 54.
[4] V. O. Key, *Southern Politics*, New York, 1950.

were not external to government, exerting 'pressure' on it but were part of the process of governance, often implementing policies as well helping to shape them. This blurring of the lines between government and interest groups went further in some nations than in others. However, the idea that a rigid line could be drawn between interest groups and government proved to be mistaken.

Neither is it clear that interest groups confine themselves to narrow or specific topics. Even interest groups which focus on a single topic, such as the environment or the dangers of nuclear war are likely to find themselves involved in wide-ranging debates. Yet other interest groups adopt policy positions on an enormous variety of subjects. As noted above, unions are particularly likely to take policy stands on almost every important issue of the day from foreign policy to child care. This breadth of interest is found in the United States in a variety of other organizations. The tendencies of the major farmers' organizations in the United States to take often very controversial stands on topics such as whether to allow the United Nations to remain on American soil, national health insurance and civil rights policy has been noted elsewhere.[5] Nor are the broad policy stands taken by American interest groups mere paper stands; American interest groups often do become swept up in wide ranging coalitions of interest groups promoting or opposing policies, Supreme Court appointments or the ratification of treaties.[6] In contrast, some interest groups, even though their members may be closely identified with one particular party, do maintain the very clear distinction between interest group activities and party politics which we had initially expected. Both the CBI and NFU in Britain, for example, maintain a focus on the details of government policy even though their members have a strong electoral attachment to the Conservatives. We should also recognize that some political parties have very narrow concerns, particularly in political systems with proportional representation so that parties can have real power with a small

[5] Graham K. Wilson, *Special Interests and Policymaking*, John Wiley and Sons, Chichester, 1977.

[6] For a lively account of the conflict over the nominations to the Supreme Court by President Nixon of Judges Haynsworth and Carswell, see Richard Harris, *Decision*, Ballantine Books, New York, 1971.

share of the vote if strategically located when coalitions are formed/ Thus the Swedish Agrarian Party used to focus on advancing the interests of farmers and the Israeli religious parties are concerned with even narrower, if extreme, concerns. In short, both interest groups and political parties vary in how broad or narrow are their concerns.

Just as interest groups and political parties can play relatively similar or very differentiated roles, so they vary in the relationship between them. There is no single pattern of relationships between interest groups and political parties either between or within countries. The first task is to differentiate the variety of relationships between parties and interest groups which exist. In order to understand the relative differentiation or lack of differentiation between parties and interest groups, we need to examine more closely the patterns of their relationships and the forces operating on them.

One form of the relationship between interest groups and political parties is close integration. The obvious example of this pattern is provided by the relationship between Social Democratic or Labour parties and trades unions. Although the Trades Union Congress is not part of the Labour Party itself, most unions are affiliated to the party. The British Labour Party, initially created by the unions, receives the vast majority of its funds from unions and gives unions the largest single share (40 per cent) of the votes in the Electoral College which selects its leader in return. The unions also hold the vast majority of votes cast at the Annual Conference of the Labour Party which are allocated between constituency branches of the party and unions on the basis of the number of individual memberships of the Labour Party each claim. Unions have been known to increase the size of their vote at the Conference by declaring – and paying for – a larger number of party members. Unions are also important at the local level of the Labour Party, holding seats on the General Management Committees of the constituency parties. Finally, unions 'sponsor', i.e., pay retainers to a large number of Labour MPs (about half the parliamentary Labour Party) to encourage the MPs to be active on issues of concern to the unions.[7] Attempts by unions

---

[7] Grant Jordan and J. J. Richardson, *Government and Pressure Groups in Britain*, Oxford University Press, Oxford, 1987, p. 268.

to force MPs whom they sponsor to follow union policies have raised questions about the compatibility of sponsorship with the role of the MP. Indeed, the Select Committee on Privileges ruled in 1977 that threats to withdraw sponsorship from MPs who did not support union policy constituted contempt of the House of Commons. Although the Committee's concerns are understandable, it would seem odd to an American used to Political Action Committees to suggest that an interest group should continue to pay money to a legislator who opposed its policies. It might also seem more damaging to the House of Commons that an increasing number of MPs accept retainers from commercial lobbying organizations, turning themselves into 'hired guns' for contract lobbyists.

The sharpest contrast with the integration of party and interest group is the model of the non-partisan interest group. In this case, interest groups deny that they have any connection with a political party or commitment to one. A partisan commitment is seen as either inherently undesirable because it is incompatible with the professional status of the group, or unwise because close association with one party will lead to a loss of credibility with other parties and politicians. This widespread assumption, that alliance with one political party will close off other forms of political action, such as participating in policymaking through trying to persuade bureaucrats or politicians irrespective of their party allegiance, is itself debatable. After all, not only the British Trades Union Congress (itself not theoretically linked to the Labour Party) but the unions in neocorporatist countries combine support for a Social Democratic party with non-partisan participation in policymaking. None the less, many groups, such as the National Farmers' Union in Britain or the British Medical Association, clearly believe that partisan activity would destroy their influence.

Between the two extremes lies a variant of the relationship in which interest groups are political, but not partisan. Indeed, the interest groups concerned will often claim to be not merely non-partisan but actually bi-partisan, supporting candidates from at least two competing political parties. Thus, most American interest groups today are involved in supporting candidates for Congress by contributions from their political action committees (PACs). But most of these interest groups give to both Democratic and

Republican candidates, whilst even those which in practice overwhelmingly support candidates from one of the parties (e.g., the bulk of the unions) still claim to be bi-partisan and try hard to find a few candidates of the other party to support to buttress this claim of bi-partisanship. Few interest groups embrace explicitly only one political party.[8]

There is considerable variation therefore in the degree to which interest groups are joined or separated. How might this variation be explained? We have argued in chapter 5 that the character of the state plays a major role in shaping the behaviour of interest groups. States characterized by concentrated, unitary power systems are likely to encourage interest groups to rely upon technocratic lobbying. The centralized, powerful state encourages interest groups to adopt a technocratic approach, persuading decisionmakers through technocratic arguments rather than through the mobilization of political force. Indeed, overt political activity might cost the interest group effective access to policymakers who would construe its behaviour as being 'too political'. In Britain, being accepted as partner by Whitehall generally precludes being vigorously involved in electioneering.

Strong though this tendency is, not all interest groups are affected by it equally. We have noted in chapter 3 that British unions are torn between 'insider' status, i.e., participating closely and confidentially in policymaking behind the scenes, and 'outsider' status, i.e., being involved vigorously in supporting the Labour Party. Other British interest groups, such as the NFU and BMA are more obviously affected by the doctrine that insider groups must eschew open alignment with one of the political parties. No one doubts in the neocorporatist countries that unions are the allies of the Social Democrats or that business supports the 'bourgeois' parties. In Japan, the relationship between business and the bureaucracy is helped by the close relationship (especially financially) between business and the Liberal Democratic Party. Thus, electoral participation and technocratic partnership with a centralized state can coexist. Electoral activity by interest groups does not always break up partnerships with governments in centralized systems.

---

[8] For an excellent survey of political parties see Alan Ware, *Citizens, Parties and the State*, Polity Press, Cambridge, 1987 and Princeton University Press, Princeton, 1988.

In states with manifestly fragmented political systems, such as the USA, interest groups risk losing less if they are identified closely politically with either party. The existence of several different power centres (e.g., in the United States the relevant committees of the House, Senate, the relevant executive branch agency and the courts) reduces the risk that alienating one political party will make the interest group vulnerable if that party wins. Even so, some risk remains. For example, undoubtedly unions, consumer groups and environmentalists suffered a sharp reduction in their influence within the executive branch after the election of President Reagan. Some interest groups, particularly business corporations, respond to the risks which remain by pragmatically aiding both Republicans and Democrats, supporting powerful incumbent legislators, for example, rather than giving campaign contributions exclusively on the basis of ideology or party. Corporate PACs are particularly interesting because they can be seen varying their contributions according to political circumstances, giving more (following their hearts) to Republicans who have already a high probability of winning and giving to Democrats (following their heads) when the Republicans' chances are low. Yet here again, other interest groups behave differently, giving their money more or less exclusively to more liberal or more conservative politicians, even if the image of non-partisanship is maintained. The AFL-CIO and most individual unions, for example, are overwhelmingly committed to helping liberal, Democratic candidates. Only a very small number of exceptionally liberal Republicans receive campaign contributions from the AFL-CIO. In short, in fragmented as well as unitary political systems, a diversity of interest group behaviour can be seen with some groups accepting and others avoiding identification with a particular political group or party. The nature of the state alone does not determine the relationship between interest groups and political parties.

In these days when self interest is celebrated by practising politicians and the 'rational choice' political theorists as a way to understand and organize the world, it might be assumed that interest groups simply choose the optimal political strategy. The balance between electioneering and lobbying therefore reflects merely the interest group's calculation of what will best advance its interests. It is unlikely in practice, however, that interest group behaviour is so simply explained. It is certainly easy to think of examples of interest groups which might have gained more by following a different strategy than the one they adopted. Certainly, the impact of the agricultural policies of the American Farm Bureau Federation on the majority party (the Democrats) in Congress, or the industrial policies of the British TUC on the Thatcher government would have been greater had the groups been less clearly identified with a particular party and ideology. What other factors might be at work in shaping the relationship between interest groups and political parties? Three obvious factors are the character of the group's objectives, the nature of its membership and the characteristics of the group's leadership.

The connection between the nature of the *goals* of an interest group and its strategy is obvious in the case of the ties between many unions and Social Democratic parties. Rightly or wrongly, many unions seek, at least in theory, a degree of change in society which could be attained only by political means and not by industrial action alone. Indeed, many of the conflicts over strategy within the British union movement have been based not on discussions of whether or not 'insider' status during a Conservative government would produce beneficial consequences but whether or not such links would compromise the traditions and ideology of the 'Labour Movement'. Adoption of tactics which might maximize the chances of success of the interest group in what might be assumed to be its major concerns are thus handicapped by a commitment to somewhat remote ideological commitments. The nature of a group's goals affects the political strategy in a less direct manner. If an interest group is committed to seeking policies which imply an increase in government expenditure, it must expect opposition based on the costs as well as principles of its demands. The group might well be driven therefore into alliances with other similarly inclined groups to overcome anti-spending coalitions; political parties provide a forum for making such coalitions. Conversely, groups which feel that they stand to lose from an expansion of government activity will form alliances, sometimes through political parties with those similarly inclined.

The nature of an interest group's *membership* has obvious implications for the interest group's relations with political parties. Interest groups with large-scale memberships are clearly better placed to become closely associated with political parties than those which have small-scale memberships. The unions in Britain or the neocorporatist countries might feel that they claim to represent such a large sector of the population that a political party enjoying their support could win elections. There is little likelihood that a political party based on the support of a small professional group such as the Institute of Chartered Surveyors would capture many seats in parliament. Particularly in multi-party systems, it is not necessary for the interests in question to constitute something approaching a majority of the population to make the sponsorship of a political party worthwhile. One particularly interesting sector in this regard is the parties based on the support of agricultural interest groups. The Swedish Agrarian Party, as its name suggests, was based on the support of farmers. The Agrarian Party played a crucial role in the development of the modern Swedish state by supplying the votes in the Riksdag necessary to sustain Social Democratic governments. Although the links are somewhat less close, the Free Democrats in West Germany have been heavily dependent on farmers' votes and have in turn helped sustain the high subsidy policies of the Federal Republic. All the developed capitalist countries have seen the share of the population directly employed in agriculture shrink considerably, however. The former agrarian parties have been forced to broaden their appeal, as is indicated by the Swedish Agrarian Party switching its name to the Centre Party.

A further way in which the characteristics of a group's membership determines its relationship with political parties is the willingness of the membership to be directly involved in manifestly political activity. The interest groups representing professional groups have shied away from commitment to a political party. Thus the Association of University Teachers in Britain, though affiliated to the Trades Union Congress, does not affiliate to the Labour Party. The membership of the Association would support neither a commitment to the Labour Party nor what many would feel was a descent into the bullring of party politics. In contrast, some interest groups possess sufficiently committed or fanatical memberships that their leaders can throw their votes to whichever party will meet their demands. In general, political scientists have argued that interest group leaders do not control the votes of their followers; voting behaviour is shaped by a variety of more powerful influences than the instructions of an interest group leader. But some groups, such as the moral majority interest groups in the USA, can be sufficiently impassioned for their relatively small numbers of members to vote for a candidate who has promised to meet the group's major demand, such as ending abortion rights.

Finally, the characteristics of a group's membership help determine the degree to which political parties compete for its members' votes. Not all parties are likely to compete for the votes of all groups. The Labour Party is unlikely to solicit the support of shareholders. The last Republican presidential candidate to make a serious appeal for support to interest groups representing black Americans was Richard Nixon in 1960; Nixon did not repeat the strategy in his subsequent successful election campaigns in 1968 and 1972, instead using a 'southern strategy' of appealing to white voters who thought that his Democratic opponents were overly solicitous of the welfare of blacks. Farmers, in contrast, have been able to stimulate party competition for their support in many countries, and in the past have been remarkably successful in prompting parties to believe that not only is the 'farm vote' prepared to switch to the party promising the highest subsidies but that their votes will make all the difference between the success and failure of the political party. Even in Britain, where the proportion of the population employed in agriculture has long been small, there was significant competition for 'the farm vote' between the Labour, Liberal and Conservative Parties as recently as the 1960s. Undoubtedly, one reason why this competition was so easily stimulated was the nature of farmers as a group. The farmer to the Conservatives was both an entrepreneur and guardian of traditional values. The Labour Party could accept the farmer as someone who was a worker (usually employing very few people outside the family) who could be destroyed not only by the weather but by impersonal economic forces such as high interest rates. Thus both the Labour and Conservative Parties could make themselves feel comfortable about bidding for the support of this group. Not many groups have been as fortunate.

A fourth influence on the relationship between political parties and interest groups is the character of the *party system* itself. This influence is felt in a variety of ways. Political parties vary in the degree to which they are permeable by interest groups.

American political parties are perhaps the type of political party most easily influenced by outside groups, including interest groups.

Just as social movements such as Populism or the groups opposing American participation in the Vietnam War have been able to exert considerable influence within one of the political parties throughout American history, so American interest groups have been able to participate in the political parties without formally ending their claims to be non-partisan. We have noted above the extreme importance of unions as a source of funds nationally for liberal Democratic candidates. At the local level, individual unions such as the United Auto Workers in Detroit have sometimes come close to constituting the Democratic Party providing the people, money and organization to run the party. In more numerous cases, union organization as well as money has been crucial to the Democrats. In general, American political parties, possessing very few resources themselves (individual candidates raise a far higher proportion of the money and recruit a higher proportion of volunteers for campaigns than in other systems) have accepted and encouraged the involvement of interest groups in their affairs. The Republican and Democratic National Committees work closely with interest group PACs to channel money to suitable candidates. Not only have politicians solicited an increasing proportion of their funds from interest groups (so that PACs now provide about half of the funds for incumbent Representatives seeking re-election) but political parties themselves have turned to interest groups for money. In 1988, considerable publicity was given to so-called 'soft money', i.e., campaign contributions funnelled through the political parties. Soft money is much less regulated than 'hard money' going direct to the candidates. Interest groups (such as the state affiliates of the National Education Association which functions as a union for teachers) waged campaigns supposedly independent of candidates they favoured. The National Education Association also encourages its members to be nominated as delegates to national nominating conventions, although the extreme domination of the Democratic Convention in 1984 by such delegates encouraged criticism that the party was controlled by 'special interests'.

Few political parties are as quickly penetrated by interest groups as the American parties in which there is not even any real membership requirement. More formalized rules of membership and less rapidly changing power structures generally delay the growth of influence of new interest groups, though once established, groups such as unions within the British Labour Party remain powerful. The British Labour Party is a most unusual political party, however, in that it was created by interest groups (i.e., the unions). In general, the more formalized the structure of the party, the more its insulation from interest groups.

The final factor influencing the relationship between political parties and interest groups is the nature of the interest group leadership itself. It is widely known that many interest group leaders differ considerably in attitude from those they claim to represent. Union leaders in the United States are generally more liberal than union members; the ultra-conservative leadership of the American Farm Bureau Federation probably does not accurately represent American farmers when it opposed government subsidy programmes from the late 1940s until the early 1980s. As Browne remarks, 'Charles B. Shuman of the Farm Bureau emerged as a frontline spokesman for conservative economic and hawkish foreign policy decisions' showing how farm leaders could become 'leaders for causes beyond the confines of farm policy'.[9] British union leaders are generally more left wing than union members (with a minority even being supporters of the British Communist Party). Numerous factors promote the unrepresentativeness of interest group leaders. Most interest group members are relatively apathetic, perhaps because, as Olson has noted, members are often attracted to interest groups by a 'selective benefit', such as cheap insurance or the use of a grain elevator, completely unconnected to the policy objectives of the group. As the internal politics of interest groups are almost never reported in the national press and are edited out of the interest groups' own newsletters, it is hard for the rank and file to play a meaningful role. Moreover, the interest group leaders can often manipulate what information is dispensed to their own advantage; union newsletters are generally full of stories and pictures showing the leadership to the best possible advantage. Interest group leaders are probably more constrained by the threat of their

---

[9] William P. Browne, *Private Interests, Public Policy and American Agriculture*, University of Kansas Press, Lawrence, 1988, p. 198.

members leaving (what Hirschman calls 'exit'[10]) than by the internal political processes of the interest group. As many members are held in the interest group by the need to be eligible for the selective incentives which have attracted them or, in the case of union members, because where there is a closed shop one cannot leave the union without losing one's job, even 'exit' may be a less than compelling threat.

In consequence, interest group leaders generally enjoy considerable freedom to follow policies which they like, as opposed to policies which the membership approves. Many interest group leaders use this freedom to involve themselves in party politics beyond the immediate or even proximate concerns of their organizations. The use of union 'block votes' at Labour Party conferences to promote defence policies based on unilateral nuclear disarmament is a case in point. Not only was unilateral disarmament unconnected with the primary concerns of unions such as the Transport and General Workers' Union, but there was also strong evidence to suggest that its members did not even favour the policy.[11] Yet some leaders of the Union, such as Lord Cousins, achieved national prominence by their advocacy of unilateral nuclear disarmament. Similarly, in the USA, the leaders of the AFL-CIO have been prominent in conflicts within the Democratic Party concerning foreign policy; it is ironic, given the image of American unions as un-political which is still widespread, that the United Auto Workers should have left the AFL-CIO for over a decade because of conflicts over the Vietnam War. As his biographer makes clear, the long time president of the AFL-CIO, George Meany, enjoyed his prominent if unofficial position in the Democratic Party as much as Jack Jones and Hugh Scanlon enjoyed their somewhat more institutionalized prominence in the British Labour Party.[12] Thus, to put it bluntly, interest groups can be extensively involved in political parties because of the personal interests or attitudes of their leaders.

[10] Alfred O. Hirschman, *Exit, Voice and Loyalty*, Harvard University Press, Cambridge, Mass., 1970.

[11] See Ivor Crewe, 'How to win a landslide without really trying: why the Conservatives won in 1983', in Austin Ranney (ed.), *Britain at the Polls, 1983, A Study of the General Election*, American Enterprise Institute, Washington DC, 1985.

[12] Joseph Goulden, *Meany*, Athenaeum, New York, 1972.

Interest Groups or Political Parties?

In the late 1970s, some feared that political parties would lose significance and would be overshadowed by interest groups.[13] Such a development could have serious implications for the governability of western democracies. A decline in the importance of political parties and an increase in the importance of interest groups might lead to a situation in which our politics increasingly would be based on temporary coalitions built in sand. In part this view reflected the belief that interest groups are always rivals, rather than sometimes partners, sometimes rivals as we have described. In part, however, this view rested on a belief that disaggregative trends were occurring affecting both public opinion and public policy. Members of the public were increasingly concerned about focused or detailed issues such as the environment or advocating the practice of religion in schools. Simultaneously, the increased complexity of public policy has outstripped the capacity of political parties to function as policy formulating bodies.

The fear that single issue groups would displace political parties was based on a much exaggerated extrapolation of trends within the United States. The vigour of a variety of groups in the 1970s was indeed impressive. As we have seen in chapter 2, consumer, environmental, moral majority and foreign policy groups mushroomed, mobilizing citizens around all the key issues of the day. Yet, though the rise of the public interest groups was probably connected with the disillusionment with political parties which was widespread in the early 1970s, the political parties have proved resilient even in the United States. The Republican Party in particular realized that political parties could replicate many of the strategies used by interest groups, such as raising money by direct mail appeals, and could play a key role in funnelling resources from interest group PACs to the best candidates or most strategically important races. As noted above, the trend observable in the 1988 campaign seemed to be for ever larger amounts of interest money to flow to the political parties

[13] For a most useful discussion of this argument, see Ware, *Citizens, Parties and the State.*

themselves as 'soft money' contributions.

For their part, interest groups were shown to be imperfect vehicles for political participation. The yield on direct mail appeals for popular support was low, and probably declining as the supply of potential contributors to interest groups was limited and soon exhausted. Research showed that most interest groups were dependent on support from foundations, wealthy individuals or organizations such as unions or corporations which exist primarily for some non-political purpose.[14] American interest groups were also given a vivid lesson in the importance of which party controls the White House. Consumer groups saw many of their own people appointed to key regulatory posts by President Carter; after the 1980 election, President Reagan brought many business and conservative interest group officials into key posts in his administration while breaking links between executive agencies and unions, consumer and environmentalist interest groups. The tired old myth that there is no difference between the American political parties was once again refuted by the changes which President Reagan wrought. Interest groups were given a vivid lesson in the importance of the political party closest to their own policies controlling the White House and Congress. Thus any notion that the new interest groups could succeed while ignoring party or electoral politics was laid to rest.[15]

The upsurge of interest groups in the United States had not after all ended the role of political parties. In other countries, the upsurge of interest group activity was not only less conspicuous, but also even less of a challenge to the role of political parties. The Campaign for Nuclear Disarmament in Britain temporarily recovered some significance in the 1980s because of understandable fears that the Reagan administration would pursue a reckless foreign policy. Yet CND never achieved, or particularly tried to

[14] Jack Walker, 'The origins and maintenance of interest groups in America', *American Political Science Review*, 77 (1983), pp. 390–406.

[15] For some of the consequences of the Reagan victory, see Lester Salamon and Michael Lund, *The Reagan Administration and the Governing of America*, Urban Institute Press, Washington DC, 1984; C. O. Jones (ed.), *The Reagan Legacy*, Chatham House, Chatham, 1988: for the effects on regulatory agencies see Susan and Martin Tolchin, *Dismantling America, The Rush to De-Regulate*, Oxford University Press, New York, 1983; Graham K. Wilson, 'Social regulation and explanation of regulatory failure', *Political Studies*, XXXII, 2 (June 1984), pp. 203–25.

achieve, any noticeable distance from the Labour Party, whose triumph seemed to hold out the only real hope for implementation of CND's policy of unilateral British disarmament. The Greens in West Germany provided an even more interesting example. Functioning originally as an interest group so loosely structured that it was more a social movement than interest group, the Greens have become a party with representation in parliament, perhaps the most vivid example of an assessment that party politics remains more important than interest group activity. Although current splits and divisions in the Greens make it particularly difficult to describe their nature, the Greens have shown signs of adapting more to the needs of parliamentary life by ending practices such as rotating their members of the Bundestag in order to avoid the emergence of a cadre of professional politicians. It is certainly true that European and American party systems witnessed unusual instability in the 1970s and early 1980s (extensive party reforms in the United States, the break away of the Social Democrats from the British Labour Party, the rise of the French and Spanish Socialists, the loss of power by Social Democrats in Sweden and Denmark as well as the rise of the Greens in West Germany); this turmoil illustrated more the importance than the decline of party politics.

Whether or not political parties have become less relevant than interest groups because they are less able to make policy in opposition in preparation for government is also doubtful. A number of party victories in the 1970s were preceded by unusually rigorous re-examination of the details and philosophy of party policy. The Conservatives under both Heath and Thatcher made considerable efforts to re-examine party policies and doctrine while in opposition; although the Heath government abandoned many of its policy commitments in celebrated 'U turns', the Thatcher government did not. Similarly, the Reagan administration impressed many observers by its ability to 'hit the ground running' in 1981 with a series of detailed plans on how to change public policy, for example on the de-regulation of business. The greatest significance of the Thatcher and Reagan governments, however, was their illustration of how, contrary to technocratic doctrines, dramatic changes in public policy could be made not so much as a result of the re-evaluations of policy as of political will. The ability to change public policy may not, after all, be dependent as much on detailed planning in opposition as on a clear sense of direction and determination after winning the election. Moreover, an important element in the appeal of both Thatcher and Reagan might have been the simplicity of their messages in 1979 and 1980; the analogy both would draw between family and state finances was perhaps more telling than whether or not their programmes had been carefully costed.

If political parties are not being displaced by interest groups, neither is there any sign that interest groups will be displaced by political parties. The relationship between the two types of institution will continue to show the same mixture of co-operation, conflict and rivalry that has existed in the past. Interest groups will sometimes work with, sometimes work against, political parties, the balance of power between them being shaped by the varied forces we have outlined.

7

Change and Stability

What has been the purpose or value of studying interest groups for political scientists? At least two answers can be given to this question.

The first is that interest groups, like political parties, constitute a form of political participation used by millions of people and thousands of organizations in different political systems. The study of interest groups is therefore as obviously a part of political science as is the study of voting behaviour, political parties, protests or any other form of political life.

The second, and more difficult, answer to the question asserts that the study of interest groups tells us much about the relationship between government and key interests in society, especially, though not exclusively, economic interests. This answer is difficult because it inevitably raises another question: how important are interest groups in linking interests in society to government? It is easy to think of linkages between government and interests other than interest groups as such. The landed interest in Britain in the first half of the nineteenth century was not *linked* to government through interest groups; the landed interest *was* the government. Similarly, the ineffective business interest groups in the United States in the 1950s were less important in linking the Eisenhower administration to business interests than was the fact that the administration was composed of former business executives; 'eight millionaires and a plumber' was the description of Eisenhower's initial Cabinet, and the plumber (Secretary of Labor Durkin, former leader of the plumbers' union) soon resigned. Neither might interest group activity be that important in explaining which interests will dominate public policy. Lindblom, for example, believes that business enjoys a privileged position among interest groups because it can punish unco-operative governments by refusing to invest within their territory.[1] This implicit threat of an investment strike by business interests may well contribute more to influencing public policy than any of the activities of business interest groups.

Important though such qualifications are to any argument for the importance of interest groups, they do not constitute a proof that interest groups are irrelevant. As Weber noted, modern societies are characterized by an increased differentiation of functions. We are more likely today to distinguish the state from other social institutions than in the eighteenth century; we are more likely to have clearly distinguishable groups of professional politicians, bureaucrats and interest group or business executives than in the early nineteenth century. Only in the United States does the circulation of elites into the top levels of government from social institutions such as business corporations continue to be important, though as we have seen, movement in the opposite direction (i.e., from government into business) continues to be an important part of the French and Japanese systems. Even in the United States, however, few would doubt that the complexity of the modern state precludes such former business executives as Secretary of State George Schultz functioning effectively as representatives in government of their former interests; Schultz had neither the time nor the opportunity to represent his former employer, the Bechtel Corporation, in resolving its disputes with the Occupational Safety and Health Administration.

It is not surprising, therefore that the clear trend in the United States as in Europe has been for even powerful social institutions such as business to feel the need to be represented by organized interest groups. This trend has been further encouraged by the mercurial shifts in the political balance between interest groups in many countries in the 1970s. The case of business is particularly illuminating. As Vogel[2] and the present author have maintained, while it may have been plausible to argue that business in the

[1] Charles E. Lindblom, *Politics and Markets*, Basic Books, New York, 1977.

[2] David Vogel, 'The power of business in the United States: a reappraisal', *British Journal of Political Science*, 13 (1983), pp. 19–43 and Vogel's 'Political science and the study of corporate power: a dissent from the new conventional wisdom', *British Journal of Political Science*, 17 (1987), pp. 385–408. Graham K. Wilson, *Interest Groups in the United States*, Oxford University Press, Oxford and New York, 1981, esp. ch. 4.

United States did not need to exert itself politically in the 1950s, by the 1970s American business executives felt that they were losing frequently on important issues. The predictable result was that business moved quickly to improve its performance in the normal interest group game. Though radical theorists have contended that interest group activity accounts for only a small proportion of the totality of power of business in capitalist societies, for their part business executives felt strongly that increased interest group activity was vital to protect their interests. The increase in the number of PACs, corporate embassies in Washington and improvements in the quality of business organizations in the United States have been noted above. Nor were these trends confined to the United States. Concern about the attacks on business from other interest groups such as environmentalists or increasingly militant workers prompted business executives in many countries to follow their American counterparts in strengthening their capacity to influence government. It is interesting to note that a number of radical political scientists have joined other colleagues in attributing important consequences for the entire political system to this upsurge in business activity.

The obvious importance of promoting investment and economic growth for modern democratic governments does make it difficult to argue that the totality of business power is equivalent to the power of business interest groups. State and national governments around the world have vied with each other in the 1980s to prove that they have the best business climate and deserve to be the recipients of international investment. It would be difficult to argue that interest groups other than business have anything like as privileged a position as business which gives them strength irrespective of the scale or effectiveness of their political activity. Consumers, farmers, doctors, academics and, as Offe emphasizes,[3] unions, are not likely to enjoy much leverage with government unless they organize. Unfortunately, as Olson noted,[4] the logic of collective action makes it inherently more difficult and, one

[3] Claus Offe and H. Wisenthal 'The two logics of collective action: theoretical notes on social class and organisational form', in Clause Offe, *Disorganized Capitalism*.

[4] Mancur Olson, *The Logic of Collective Action: Public Goods and the Theory of Groups*, Schocken Books, New York, 1968.

might add, in practice expensive, to organize large numbers of people. It might appear that voting blocks may have influence with politicians in competitive party systems irrespective of whether or not they are organized. In practice, however, politicians are likely to be able to appease blocks of voters through symbolic actions or minor concessions unless the voting blocks are represented by interest groups which can examine the politicians' proposals thoroughly. In short, while it is today little more than a theoretical game to try to imagine what would be the power of business corporations if they were not well represented in the interest group system, it is inconceivable that all other interests could have much leverage over government without forming interest groups. Thus, the study of interest groups does indeed have much to offer the student of the general relationship between interests and government.

What questions should we ask about this relationship? It is clear that the agenda of political science has changed significantly in the last twenty years so that not only the answers given but the questions asked by political scientists have changed. The overriding concern of political scientists who studied interest groups in the 1960s was the representativeness of the interest group system. The pluralists argued that the interest group system was indeed reasonably representative because power was dispersed (though not necessarily equally) among a large number of competing interest groups, all of which had some effective capacity to shape public policy. Pluralists were attacked by critics who advanced a variety of criticisms of their argument. Power, elite theorists argued, was not widely dispersed but concentrated in the hands of a few.[5] Important common interests, such as protection of the environment, were not adequately represented because of the problems in organizing collective action identified by Olson. The interest group system was also said to be unrepresentative in that generally the wealthy participated more in the interest group system, the poor less. Moreover, the power structures of institutions would 'organize out' of consideration issues troubling to powerful institutions; Crenson argued that Gary, Indiana failed to adopt air pollution control ordinances

---

[5] C. Wright Mills, *The Power Elite*, Oxford University Press, New York, 1955.

because it was dominated by US Steel.[6] Finally, as we have seen, Lindblom argued that the interest group system was rigged in favour of business. Not only did business have unusual opportunities to play the conventional interest group game; business also had the leverage provided by the implicit or explicit threat to shift investment if government did not give it what it wanted.

The debate between the pluralists and their critics prompted, somewhat strangely, much research on local government in the United States and little research on interest groups in national government. The controversy, perhaps like many in political science, faded away rather than being resolved. Perhaps to some extent events played their part in this. After the shocks to the American political system of controversies over race, Vietnam and Watergate, prominent pluralists such as Dahl or Lindblom became much more critical of the power structure, while radicals became less fatalistic about the possibilities of taking on the power structure.

In part, however, the debate between pluralists and their critics became irresolvable of a conflict between them over the definition of power. The most influential of the attacks on pluralism included some notion that the most effective, pernicious forms of the exercise of power were based on a type of power that was not directly, empirically observable. Steven Lukes, and to some degree Lindblom, argued that the most powerful interests in our society have the capacity to shape the definition of their interests by other groups in society; business can cause consumers and workers to define their interests in practice in a form compatible with business's interests.[7] As groups whose true interests clashed with business failed to apprehend their true interests, conflict was avoided. In contrast, pluralists argued or assumed that the exercise of power involved the observable changing of behaviour so that A caused B to undertake something B would not otherwise have done. Interests were autonomously and accurately defined by members of groups; it was not for the observer to say whether or not groups were accurately or falsely conscious of their interests. Once the dispute between the pluralists and their critics

---

[6] Matthew Crenson, *The Unpolitics of Air Pollution: A Study of Non-Decisionmaking in the Cities*, John Hopkins University Press, Baltimore and London, 1971.

[7] Steven Lukes, *Power, a Radical View*, Macmillan, London, 1974.

had reached this level, little could be done to resolve it, for the question of whether groups understood or misunderstood their interests was dependent for its answer on the fundamental beliefs of the antagonists about the nature of society or human beings. Naturally, there was little agreement on these issues either.

Even within the pluralist tradition, however, power turned out to be as difficult as it was an obvious focus for research. The obvious tactic for studying interest group power, the case study, was criticized on the grounds that a study of the power of an interest on one type of issue did not predict the interest's power in another policy area. Yet the resources required to carry out multiple case studies crossing policy areas would be beyond most researchers. It is rare to see a full test of interest group power. Interest groups rarely engaged in full battle against each other anticipating the power or reactions of each other. Participants in interest group conflicts frequently advanced explanations other than interest group pressure to explain their actions leaving the observer little scope in practice to contest their explanations; American legislators voting as their campaign contributors would wish usually argue that their vote was cast to serve the public or constituency's interest, not to please the PAC. Reputational surveys, in which those thought to be powerful were asked to single out those people they thought to be particularly powerful, avoided some of these methodological difficulties, but seemed inadequate themselves. In short, apart from the methodological problems, power seemed in practice to be an unhelpful focus for interest group studies.

The De-Americanizing of Interest Group Studies

Nothing has changed the questions asked in interest group studies as much as the realization that models developed to fit the United States and the questions asked by or through them are not appropriate for other countries. As in most, if not all, branches of empirical political science, studies of interest groups and their activities took place far earlier in the United States than in other countries; moreover, Britain, the next most studied country, had an interest group system which, though different from the

American model, was not as radically different as other examples we have encountered.

The unique features of the American interest group system which temporarily misled students of interest groups in general can be summarized easily. As we have seen, the American interest group system was unusually *fragmented*, with weak peak associations to represent business, labour or agriculture in general, and below that level even more narrowly focused organizations such as trade associations were weak. Interest groups were meant to be differentiated from the state, and when through elite circulation or interaction, or through 'iron triangles' the boundaries between the state and interest groups seemed to be breached, this was seen as cause for concern. Finally, at least in theory, interest groups were supposed to be not only autonomous but auto-generating; again, when examples of the state creating interest groups or strengthening them were discovered, the examples were generally assumed to be both unusual and cause for concern.

Increased interest in continental Europe and Japan, perhaps as a result of their economic successes in the 1960s and 1970s, revealed very different types of interest group systems. In extreme contrast to the United States stood the neocorporatist systems. In place of fragmented, competing interest groups, neocorporatist interest group systems were characterized by more limited numbers of groups, each having an effective monopoly of representation within its sphere. Peak associations were strong, and generally had affiliated to them the more specialized, subordinate groups such as unions or trade associations, which in turn enjoyed a monopoly within their spheres. The assumption of interest group autonomy and spontaneous auto-creation which dominated thinking about interest groups in Britain and the United States was supported neither normatively nor in practice elsewhere. Interest groups were assumed to be, and generally were, licensed if not created by the state, which endowed them with a monopoly of the right to represent the interest for which they spoke. While important differences between countries existed in the degree of neocorporatism, and in the interests represented (so that labour was not part of the neocorporatist policymaking practices of Japan and France while it was in Scandinavia), it seemed that on balance the United States was not the prototype of interest group systems around the world, but very much an exception, occupying an extreme position on charts of the degree to which countries were neocorporatist.

The recognition that the American interest group system was exceptional rather than typical prompted political scientists to ask different questions about interest group systems. The traditional question asked in research on American interest groups was whether they enhanced or diminished the representativeness of the policymaking process. Did interest groups enhance partici-pation, or was the degree of inequality within the interest group system so extreme that it exacerbated inequalities of political influence? Did interest groups collectively promote the common good as they competed with each other (as the market supposedly promotes consumer satisfaction) or did they subvert the common good as they pursued selfish goals? In contrast, the question which Schmitter raised about interest group systems was not so much about their representativeness, or about the distribution of power within them. It was more about the contribution which interest group systems made to the *efficiency* of political econom-ies. Neocorporatist interest group systems promoted economic growth, full employment and stability. Pluralist interest group systems failed to achieve these objectives. Indeed, as Olson suggested, pluralist interest group systems might be an actual impediment to growth, particularly in countries such as Britain where long periods of political stability had allowed interest groups to consolidate their position. A number of studies of regulation suggested that neocorporatist interest group systems facilitated the smooth, efficient and reasonable pursuit of goals which in more pluralist interest group systems produced conflict, stalemate and either unreasonably onerous or ineffective regu-lation. Advocates of industrial policies in the United States hoped to be able to emulate the economic benefits which they believed a partnership between interest groups and government had secured in other countries. Thus, the debate now focused on the efficiency rather than the representativeness of interest group systems.

Obviously this change of focus for political scientists reflected changes in popular concerns. The issue of economic competitive-ness has been tremendously important in many countries. The great concern in Britain in the 1970s about the reasons for the country's industrial failure had its counterpart in the United States in the 1980s. In many countries the distributive questions which had dominated political debate in the 1960s and 1970s (who gets what, and what should they get?) gave way to debates about how most efficaciously to increase economic growth or reduce unemployment. The switch in the dominant concern of interest group studies away from representation and towards economic efficiency parallels this wider change in political debate.

A second change related to the growth of a more sophisticated comparative perspective on interest groups has been the revival of interest in the factors shaping interest group systems, including the role of the state. If interest group systems were very different in different countries, what had made them so? Obviously a number of answers to this question had always been implicit in the literature. For example, the reasons why class consciousness is greater in many European countries than in the United States, with obvious implications for the strength of unions, had been the subject of discussion since the nineteenth century receiving attention from many major writers, most notably Sombart. One of the ways in which American political scientists celebrated the superiority of the American civic culture was by arguing that Americans were more likely to participate in interest groups than other peoples, although as we have seen, this is not true of economic groups.

The comparative perspective, combined with the considerable interest in neocorporatist interest group systems, made the role of the state in shaping interest group systems more obvious. If, as neocorporatist writers argued, in many countries monopolistic interest groups were created or licensed by the state, the role of the state was clearly more important than if, as the American pluralists had assumed, interest groups emerged spontaneously and independently of the state. Yet the role of the state could be appreciated fully only by not only bearing in mind the conscious building up or tearing down of particular interest groups, such as the promotion of the FNSEA by the French state, but appreciating the degree to which the state unconsciously structured interest groups, along with most other institutions. The Constitution, the laws and legal traditions and the balance of power between different institutions within the state all made an impact on the interest group system. It is no coincidence that the fragmented American state coexists with a fragmented interest group system.

Yet if we have brought the state back in to explain differences in interest group systems, it would surely be unwise to drive all other factors out. Political culture, itself the product of the history of a nation, class consciousness, religious controversy, regional, ethnic and racial divisions all play a part in shaping interest group systems. Recognizing the role of the state should not cause us to overlook these factors. Indeed, states, like people in Marx's famous aphorism, make their own history but they make their own history within limits; and states, similarly, make their own interest group systems within limits. The Swedish and Norwegian states, for example, did not simply go out and decide to be neocorporatist; they became neocorporatist in the context of seeking a solution to the problem of reconciling an extraordinarily strong union system with a considerable dependency on foreign trade. Neocorporatism offered a solution compatible with these constraints and was not merely a policy option chosen for abstract reasons.

We might conclude therefore that the de-Americanization of interest group studies has served to highlight both the variety of interest group systems and the varieties of factors shaping those systems. While disagreeing about the relative importance of explanatory factors, we can agree that interest group systems vary, and that there is no one interest group system which is the product of modernization, industrialization or any of the other common experiences of the western democracies.

Change within Interest Group Systems

Yet not only do the questions and answers of political scientists change, so too do interest group systems. The relative standing of interest groups can certainly change over time. The change in the political strength of business and labour in the United States is a case in point. Thirty years ago, most Washington observers would have said that the unions, particularly through the AFL-CIO had much better lobbyists, electoral campaign machinery and larger funds from which to provide campaign contributions than had business. By the mid-1980s, the situation had been reversed. Similarly, public interest groups representing consumers or environmentalists were either non-existent or much weaker in the United States in the early 1960s than they were in the late 1960s or early 1970s. Most observers believe that American public interest groups then lost influence to business in the late 1970s and 1980s.

We have little sense of how rapidly interest group systems change. It may well be that the degree of change in the American interest group system in the 1960s and 1970s was quite unusual, and was due either to the nature of the times or the nature of the American political system. It is certainly possible that the interest group system of the United States changes more rapidly than the interest group systems of other countries because it is less institutionalized in its linkages to government. Interest groups in the United States tend not to have as closely defined relations with bureaucracies, political parties or politicians as do interest groups in other countries. The relations of interest groups with other actors can therefore change more readily than in other countries. None the less, change does occur in other interest group systems. The somewhat one-sided partnership between British unions and the Labour government in the 1970s made union leaders more influential than they had been in the past, or would be in the future. The neocorporatist systems, as we have noted, showed much less stability in the 1980s than they had in the 1960s. Yet in general, the more structured the interest group/government relations, the more slowly they change. Major changes in interest groups involved in neocorporatist systems or their relative power probably occur only because of major crises.

Interest group systems can also change because of changes in the political system more generally. A diminished interest in participating in political parties in the United States in the 1960s created new opportunities for public interest groups to marshal support. An interventionist government seeking to combine low inflation with full employment through an incomes policy has greater need of the co-operation of interest groups than has a government such as Thatcher's trying to disengage from detailed intervention in the economy. It has been argued that the British are changing culturally in a way which leads to reduced interest in collective activities, such as attending soccer matches or playing team games, and increased interest in individualistic forms of activity, such as fishing or watching movies at home on the VCR.

Such a cultural change would have obvious implications for the degree of identification individuals make with 'their' interest group. We have encountered similar arguments that neocorporatism is a victim of its own success because differential opportunities for prosperity in different economic sectors undermine the class solidarity on which neocorporatist arrangements rest.

Thus, although the rate of change in the American interest group system may be unusually great, it is by no means the case that only the American interest group system changes. It would seem, therefore, that there is little likelihood of stability in the questions and answers which political scientists generate about interest groups. Changes in the interest group systems themselves, in the political economies in which they are embedded and in the concerns which motivate political scientists will almost certainly continue to produce changes in writing on interest groups in the future. The economic upturn of the 1980s may well encourage greater interest again in the distribution of power and wealth as the difficulties of wealth creation recede.

Awareness of the variety of interest group systems discussed in this book will enhance awareness of the possibilities for change. It has been easy to argue that industrial or post-industrial societies are all characterized by similar forces prompting the growth of interest groups, or increased government dependence on them. In fact, there is, as we have noted, considerable variation in the interest group systems of democracies. Neither is there any sign that the interest group systems of the advanced countries are converging. The Swedish interest group system shows few signs of becoming similar to the American interest group system. Indeed, it is possible that both highly neocorporatist and highly pluralist interest group systems may be compatible with economic success; as Goldthorpe suggests, the American and neocorporatist models may be two alternative paths into the future.

The existence of different forms of interest group system will inevitably encourage policymakers to wonder whether they can change their own interest group system into something better. This book suggests caution. Interest group systems can be changed to some degree by policymakers. Individual interest groups can be built up or reduced, by encouraging or ending the effective monopoly of representation an interest group has enjoyed. Interest groups can be given greater or lesser access to policymakers. Yet for all that, interest group systems are shaped by the unique combinations of state structures, political cultures, and histories which vary from country to country. It is a mistake to imagine that there is only one type of interest group system in the world; it is also a mistake to assume that a country's interest group system can be changed at will to promote policy goals. Attempts to mould the British interest group system into a more neocorporatist form in the 1960s and 1970s had a limited effect. The complexity of factors shaping interest group systems means that although policymakers may change interest group systems somewhat, they do so within limits.

We have concluded this book by emphasizing the variety of interest group systems, both between different countries and, over time, within the same country. An emphasis on the variety of interest group systems produced by differing cultures, state structures and historical experiences contrasts with an increasingly popular approach to the study of interest groups which tends to ignore such differences. This approach is the rational choice school, which shares many of its assumptions of rational utility maximization by individuals with micro-economics. Political science has been passing through a period in which the alleged intellectual successes of economics have encouraged a tendency to adopt rational choice approaches which rest on assumptions which most students of comparative politics would reject. Rational choice approaches to the study of interest groups either assume a uniformity of human motivations or cope with complexity by redescribing reality in simplistic terms; people either maximize material gain or they must be maximizing some psychic satisfaction by joining interest groups. Such simplistic assumptions have far less to contribute to the study of politics, rooted in many different human aspirations, than to the study of economics. Indeed, the most astute writers influenced by the rational choice tradition such as James Q. Wilson and Terry Moe have been eager to emphasize the variety of reasons for joining interest groups. A comparative perspective on interest groups makes one aware of even greater differences in the representation of interests. Similar groups, such as unions, not only define the interests of their members very differently in, say, the United States and Sweden, but pursue those interests very differently in, for example, Austria and Great Britain. The real world of interest group politics is much more varied, fascinating and, indeed, political than rational choice theory pretends. Of course it is the duty of the political scientist to search for pattern and meaning in the midst of variety. The quest can be pursued successfully, however, only by setting aside reliance on simplified assumptions about human behaviour characteristic of rational choice theory and accepting the contribution of a variety of cultural, institutional and historical explanations.

Bibliography

Almond, Gabriel, 'Corporatism, pluralism and professional memory', *World Politics*, 35 (1983), pp. 245–60.

Almond, Gabriel, 'A return to the state', with replies by Eric Nordlinger, Theodore Lowi and Sergio Fabbrini, *APSR*, 82 (1988), pp. 853–904.

Almond, Gabriel and Verba, Sidney, *The Civic Culture: Political Attitudes and Democracy in Five Nations*, Princeton University Press, Princeton, 1963.

Bachrach, Peter and Baratz, Morton, *Power and Poverty: Theory and Practice*, Oxford University Press, Oxford and New York, 1970.

Badie, Bertrand and Birnbaum, Pierre, *The Sociology of the State*, University of Chicago Press, Chicago, 1983.

Bauer, Raymond, Pool, Ithiel de Sola and Dexter, Lewis Anthony, *American Business and Public Policy: The Politics of Foreign Trade*, Atherton Press, New York, 1963.

Beer, Samuel, *Modern British Politics*, Faber and Faber, London, 1965 and 1969.

Beer, Samuel, *Britain Against Itself*, Faber and Faber, London, 1982.

Berger, Suzanne (ed.), *Organizing Interests in Western Europe*, Cambridge University Press, Cambridge and New York, 1981.

Berry, Jeffrey, *The Interest Group Society*, Little Brown, Boston, 1984.

Birbaum, Jeffrey H. and Murray, Alan S., *Showdown at Gucci Gulch: lawmakers, lobbyists and the unlikely triumph of tax reform*, Random House, New York, 1987.

Birch, Anthony, 'Overload, ungovernability and delegitimation', *BJPolS*, 14 (1984), pp. 135–60.

Block, Fred, 'The ruling class does not rule: notes on the marxist theory of the state', *Socialist Review*, 33 (1977), pp. 5–23.

Browne, William P., *Private Interests, Public Policy and American Agriculture*, University of Kansas Press, Lawrence, 1988.

Caldeira, Gregory and Wright, John, 'Organized interests and agenda setting in the US Supreme Court', *APSR*, 82 (1988), pp. 1109–28.

Campbell, John, 'Compensation for expatriates: a case study of interest group politics and party government negotiation', in T. J. Pempel (ed.), *Policymaking in Contemporary Japan*, Cornell University Press, Ithaca, 1977.

Carnoy, Martin, *The State and Political Theory*, Princeton University Press, Princeton, 1984.

Chubb, John, *Interest Groups and the Bureaucracy*, Stanford University Press, Stanford, 1983.

Cohen, Stephen, *Modern Capitalist Planning: the French Model*, Harvard University Press, Cambridge, Mass., 1969.

Crenson, Matthew, *The Unpolitics of Air Pollution: a Study of Non-Decisionmaking in the Cities*, Johns Hopkins University Press, Baltimore and London, 1971.

Dahl, Robert, *A Preface to Democratic Theory*, University of Chicago Press, Chicago, 1956.

Dahl, Robert, *Who Governs?*, Yale University Press, New Haven, 1961.

Dahl, Robert, *Dilemmas of Pluralist Democracy*, Yale University Press, New Haven, 1982.

Dennis, Jack, 'Groups and political behavior: legitimation, deprivation and competing values', *Political Behavior*, 9 (1987), pp. 323–71.

Destler, I. M., *American Trade Politics: System Under Stress*, Institute for International Economics, Washington DC, and the Twentieth Century Fund, New York, 1986.

Donnelly, Michael, 'Setting the price of rice: a study in political decisionmaking', in T. J. Pempel (ed.), *Policymaking in Contemporary Japan*, Cornell University Press, Ithaca, 1977.

Eckstein, Harry, *Pressure Politics: the Case of the BMA*, University of California Press, Berkeley, 1963.

Einhom, Eric and Logue, John, *Welfare States in Hard Times: Problems, Policy and Politics in Denmark and Norway*, Kent Popular Press, Kent, Ohio, 1982.

Evans, Peter, Rueschemeyer, Dietrich and Skocpol, Theda (eds), *Bringing the State Back In*, Cambridge University Press, Cambridge and New York, 1985.

Finer, S. E., *Anonymous Empire*, Pall Mall Press, London, 1966.

Gais, Thomas, Peterson, M. and Walker, J., 'Interest groups, iron triangles and representative government in American national government', *BJPolS*, 14 (1984), pp. 161–86.

Garson, G. David, *Group Theories of Politics*, Sage Publications, Beverly Hills, 1978.

Gerlich, Peter, 'Government structure', in Kurt Steiner (ed.), *Modern Austria*, Society for the Promotion of Science and Scholarship, Palo Alto, California, 1981.

Goldthorpe, John, (ed.) *Organising Interests in Western Europe*, Cambridge University Press, Cambridge and New York, 1981.

Grant, Wyn, (ed.), *The Political Economy of Corporatism*, Macmillan, Houndmills and London, 1985.

Grant, Wyn, (with Jane Sargent), *Business and Politics in Britain*, Macmillan, London, 1987.

Grant, Wyn and Marsh, David, *The CBI*, Hodder and Stoughton, London, 1977.

Greenstone, J. David, *Labor in American Politics*, University of Chicago Press, Chicago, 1977.

Habermas, Jurgen, *Legitimation Crisis*, tr. Thomas McCarthy, Beacon Press, Boston, 1975, and Heinemann, London, 1976.

Hamilton, Alexander, Madison, James and Jay, John, *The Federalist Papers*, edited by Willmoore Kendall and George Carey, Arlington House, New Rochelle, 1966.

Hayes, Michael, *Lobbyists and Legislators: A Theory of Political Markets*, Rutgers University Press, New Brunswick, 1986.

Heclo, Hugh and Madsen, Henrik, *Policy and Politics in Sweden*, Temple University Press, Philadelphia, 1987.

Hertzke, Alan, *Representing God in Washington*, University of Tennessee Press, Knoxville, 1988.

Hirschman, A. O., *Exit, Voice and Loyalty*, Harvard University Press, Cambridge, Mass., 1970.

Jessop, Bob, 'Recent theories of the capitalist state', *Cambridge Journal of Economics*, 1 (1977), pp. 353–73.

Jessop, Bob, *The Capitalist State: Theory and Methods*, New York University Press, New York, 1982.

Johnson, Chalmers, *MITI and the Japanese Miracle: The Growth of Industrial Policy, 1925–75*, Stanford University Press, Stanford, 1982.

Jordan, Grant and Richardson, J. J., *Government and Pressure Groups in Britain*, Oxford University Press, Oxford, 1987.

Katzenstein, Peter, *Small States in World Markets*, Cornell University Press, Ithaca, 1985.

Kaufman, Herbert, *The Administrative Behavior of Federal Bureau Chiefs*, Brookings Institution, Washington DC, 1981.

Keeler, John, *The Politics of Neocorporatism in France*, Oxford University Press, Oxford and New York, 1987.

King Anthony (ed.), *Why is Britain Becoming Harder to Govern?*, BBC Publications, London, 1976.

King, Anthony (ed.), *The New American Political System*, American Enterprise Institute, Washington DC, 1978.

Kingdon, John, *Congressmen's Voting Decisions*, Harper and Row, New York, 1973.

Kornberg, Alan, *The Politics of Mass Society*, The Free Press, Glencoe, 1959.

Kumar, Martha Joynt and Grossman, Michael Baruch, 'The presidency and interest groups', in Michael Nelson (ed.), *The Presidency and the Political System*, C. Q. Press, Washington DC, 1984.

Kvavik, Robert, *Interest Groups in Norwegian Politics*, Universitetsforlaget, Oslo, 1976.

Lehmbruch, Gerhard and Schmitter, Philippe (eds), *Patterns of Corporatist Policymaking*, Sage Publications, London and Beverly Hills, 1982.

Lindblom, Charles E., *Politics and Markets: the World's Political Economic Systems*, Basic Books, New York, 1977.

Lowi, Theodore, *The End of Liberalism*, 2nd edn, W. W. Norton, New York, 1979.

Lukes, Steven, *Power, A Radical View*, Macmillan, London, 1974.

MacArthur, J. H. and Scott, B. R., *Industrial Planning in France*,

Harvard University Press, Cambridge, Mass., 1969.

McFarland, Andrew, *Public Interest Lobbies*, AEI, Washington DC, 1976.

McFarland, Andrew, *Common Cause, Lobbying in the Public Interest*, Chatham House, Chatham, 1984.

Marin, Bernd, 'Austria – the paradigm case of liberal corporatism?', in Wyn Grant (ed.), *The Political Economy of Corporatism*, Macmillan, Houndmills, 1985.

Marsh, David and Locksley, Gareth, 'Capital in Britain: its structural power and influence over policy', *Western European Politics*, 6, 2, (April 1983), pp. 36–60.

Matthews, Donald, *US Senators and their World*, University of North Carolina Press, Chapel Hill, 1960.

Milbrath, Lester, *The Washington Lobbyists*, Rand McNally, Chicago, 1963.

Moe, Terry, *The Organization of Interests*, University of Chicago Press, Chicago, 1980.

Moran, Michael, 'Finance capital and pressure group politics', *BJPolS*, 11 (1981), pp. 381–404.

Nie, Norman and Verba, Sidney, *Participation in America*, Harper and Row, New York, 1972.

Nordlinger, Eric, *On the Autonomy of the Democratic State*, Harvard University Press, Cambridge, Mass., 1981.

O'Connor, James, *The Fiscal Crisis of the State*, St Martin's Press, New York, 1971.

Offe, Claus, 'The attribution of public status to interest groups', in Suzanne Berger (ed.), *Organizing Interests in Western Europe*, Cambridge University Press, Cambridge, 1981, pp. 123–58.

Offe, Claus and Wisenthal, H., 'The two logics of collective action: theoretical notes on social class and organisational form', *Political Power and Social Theory*, 1, pp. 67–115. 1985.

Offe, Claus, *Disorganized Capitalism*, MIT Press, Cambridge, Mass., 1985.

Olsen, Johann, *Organized Democracy: Political Institutions in a Welfare State*, Universitetsforlaget, Oslo, 1983.

Olson, Mancur, *The Logic of Collective Action: Public Goods and the*

Theory of Groups, Schocken Books, New York, 1968.

Olson, Mancur, *The Rise and Decline of Nations, Economic Growth, Stagflation, and Social Rigidities*, Yale University Press, New Haven, 1982.

Orren, Karen, 'Standing to sue: interest group conflict in the federal courts', *APSR*, 70, 3 (September 1976), pp. 723–41.

Pratt, Henry, *The Gray Lobby*, University of Chicago Press, Chicago, 1976.

Presthus, Robert, *Elite Accommodation in Canadian Politics*, Cambridge University Press, Cambridge and New York, 1973.

Rokkan, Stein, 'Norway, numerical democracy and corporate pluralism', in Robert Dahl, (ed.), *Political Oppositions in Western Democracies*, Yale University Press, New Haven, 1966.

Rousseau, Jean-Jacques, *The Social Contract* (with an introduction by Sir Ernest Barker), Oxford University Press, Oxford and New York, 1966.

Sabato, Larry, *PAC Power*, W. W. Norton, New York, 1984.

Salisbury, Robert, 'An exchange theory of interest groups', *Midwest Journal of Political Science*, 13, 1 (1969), pp. 64–78.

Salisbury, Robert, 'Interest representation – the dominance of institutions', *APSR* 78, 1 (1984) pp. 64–76.

Salisbury, Robert, Heinz, John P., Laumann, Edward O. and Nelson, Robert L., 'Who works with whom? interest group alliances and opposition', *APSR*, 81 (1987), pp. 1217–34.

Samuels, Richard J., *The Business of the Japanese State: Energy Markets in Comparative and Historical Perspective*, Cornell University Press, Ithaca, 1987.

Sapiro, Virginia, 'When are interests interesting?', *APSR*, 75, 3 (1981), pp. 701–16.

Schattschneider, E. E., *The Semi-Sovereign People: A Realist's View of Democracy*, Holt, Reinhart and Winston, New York, 1960.

Schattschneider, E. E., *Politics, Pressures and the Tariff*, reprint, Arno Press, New York, 1974 (original 1935).

Schlozman, Kay Lehman and Tierney, John, *Organized Interests and American Democracy*, Harper and Row, New York, 1986.

Schmitter, Philippe, 'Still the century of corporatism?', *Review of Politics*, 36 (1974), pp. 85–131.

Schmitter, Philippe, 'Modes of interest intermediation and models of societal change in western Europe', *Comparative Political Studies*, 10 (1977), pp. 7–38.

Schmitter, Philippe, 'Regime stability and systems of interest intermediation in western Europe and North America', in Suzanne Berger (ed.), *Organizing Interests in Western Europe*, Cambridge University Press, Cambridge and New York, 1981.

Schmitter, Philippe and Lehmbruch, Gerhard, *Trends Toward Corporatist Intermediation*, Sage Publications, London and Beverly Hills, 1979.

Self, Peter and Storing, Herbert, *The State and the Farmer*, Allen and Unwin, London, 1962 and 1971.

Shapiro, Martin, 'The Supreme Court's "return" to economic regulation', *Studies in American Political Development*, vol. 1, Yale University Press, New Haven and London, 1986.

Stepan, Alfred, *State and Society: Peru in Comparative Perspective*, Princeton University Press, Princeton, 1978.

Stewart, Richard, 'The reformation of American administrative law', *Harvard Law Review*, 88 (8) 1667–1813 (1975).

Streeck, Wolfgang, *Industrial Relations in West Germany*, Heinemann Educational, London, 1984.

Tocqueville, Alexis de, *De la Démocratie en Amérique*, Bordas, Paris, 1973.

Truman, David, *The Governmental Process*, Alfred Knopf, New York, 1951.

Useem Michael, *The Inner Circle: Large Corporations and the Rise of Political Activity in the USA and UK*, Oxford University Press, New York, 1984.

Vogel, David, 'The power of business in the United States, a Reappraisal', *BJPolS*, 13 (1983), pp. 19–43.

Vogel, David, *National Styles of Regulation*, Cornell University Press, Ithaca, 1986.

Vogel, David, 'Political science and the study of corporate power: a dissent from the new conventional wisdom', *BJPolS*, 17 (1987), pp. 385–408.

Walker, Jack, 'The origins and maintenance of interest groups in America', *APSR*, 77, 2 (1983), pp. 390–406.

Ware, Alan, *Citizens, Parties and the State*, Polity Press, Cambridge, 1987, and Princeton University Press, Princeton, 1988.

Wills, Gary, *Explaining America*, Doubleday, Garden City New Jersey, 1976.

Wilson, Graham K., *Special Interests and Policymaking: Agricultural Politics and Policies in Britain and the United States*, John Wiley and Sons, Chichester and London, 1977.

Wilson, Graham K., *Unions in American National Politics*, Macmillan, London and New York, 1979.

Wilson, Graham K., *Interest Groups in the United States*, Oxford University Press, Oxford and New York, 1981.

Wilson, Graham K., *The Politics of Safety and Health*, Oxford University Press, Oxford and New York, 1985.

Wilson, James Q., *Political Organizations*, Basic Books, New York, 1974.

Wilson, James Q., (ed.), *The Politics of Regulation*, Basic Books, New York, 1983.

Winkler, J., 'The coming corporatism', in R. Skidelsky (ed.), *The End of the Keynesian Era*, Macmillan, London, 1977.

Zeigler, L. Harman, 'Interest groups in the American states', in Virginia Gray, Herbert Jacobs and Kenneth Vines (eds), *Politics in the American States*, Little Brown, Boston, 1983, pp. 97–131.

Zysman, John, *Governments, Markets and Growth*, Cornell University Press, Ithaca, 1983.

Index